Breathe through This

Breathe through This

MINDFULNESS FOR
PARENTS OF TEENAGERS

Eline Snel

SHAMBHALA
Boston & London
2015

Shambhala Publications, Inc.
Horticultural Hall
300 Massachusetts Avenue
Boston, Massachusetts 02115
www.shambhala.com

© 2014 by Eline Snel
English translation ©2015 by Shambhala Publications, Inc.
Ruimte geven en dichtbij zijn was originally published in the
Netherlands by Uitgeverij Ten Have. www.uitgeverijtenhave.nl

9 8 7 6 5 4 3 2 1

First English-language Edition
Printed in the United States of America

⊗ This edition is printed on acid-free paper that meets
the American National Standards Institute Z39.48 Standard.
♻ This book is printed on 30% postconsumer recycled paper.
For more information please visit www.shambhala.com.

Distributed in the United States by Penguin Random House LLC
and in Canada by Random House of Canada Ltd

Designed by Lora Zorian

Library of Congress Cataloging-in-Publication Data
Snel, Eline.
Breathe through This: mindfulness for parents of teenagers/
Eline Snel.—First edition.
pages   cm
ISBN 978-1-61180-246-7 (paperback)
1. Parent and teenager. 2. Parenting—Psychological aspects.
3. Meditation. 4. Mind and body. I. Title.
HQ799.15.S666 2015
306.874—dc23
2014047503

33614056441800

Your task is not to seek for love, but merely to seek and find all the barriers within yourself that you have built against it.

Rumi

This book is dedicated to my five grandchildren: Finn, Bow, Noosa, Neel, and Nesta. Beautiful teenagers in the making!

CONTENTS

INTRODUCTION

All of us looking after and raising children know it is a big adventure in every way. And there is only one certainty: you never know what is going to happen. When you are looking after another person, you come up against the challenge of adjusting your own desires, expectations, strong emotions, and boundaries. Life with teenagers can be particularly stressful, because they do not always stick to our programs, forcing us to find a balance between their needs and our own.

This following scene may feel familiar to you:

One day, I notice my thirteen-year-old son is up surprisingly early. I usually have to drag him out of bed or encourage him by saying, "I'm driving past school anyway, would you like a lift?" But today he emerges freshly showered and smelling of green apples ("wrong shower gel," he mutters).

"What are you up to?" I ask cheerfully, but with a vague sense of unease about his fresh appearance at this early hour.

"I'm going to the doctor. I've got an appointment at eight."

"The doctor? What for? There's nothing wrong, is there?" I suddenly feel extremely anxious. Meanwhile my son eats his toast, quickly and without chewing.

"Nothing wrong? Everything's wrong." His voice is loud and strident. "You don't get it, as usual. You're so stupid! I'm going to the doctor to have my DNA tested, because I can't believe you're really my mother!"

Shocked at this outright denial of my maternal love and our unmistakable shared DNA, I look at him. "You're going to do what?"

"See what I mean? I'm not telling you again, because you never listen!"

Before I have a chance to say something about the properties of DNA, he slams the kitchen door shut. He gets his bike out of the shed and jumps on. I watch his narrow back recede. The morning got off to such a peaceful start, but now suddenly I find myself in a maelstrom of unexpected emotions.

Here I am, surrounded by granola, yogurt, and peanut butter. I want to react—immediately and impulsively. I want to tell him that I am going to the doctor too. The appointment was made a long time ago. I am also having my DNA tested, because I cannot believe he is my son. I feel like being unreasonable, like slamming the door, going after him, and yelling unashamedly: "Hey you, stop right there! I want you to listen to me!" But I don't. I stay where I am and take a time-out.

A time-out, or the ability to stop reacting right away, is the first step toward mindful living with teenagers. On so many *occasions it has helped me avoid getting sucked into feelings of powerlessness, anger, or the fear that things will not work out. From time to time it has also allowed me to escape my weary maternal head. Instead of worrying about the rapid and sudden changes in my son's behavior, I allowed myself to reconnect with my body. Breathing in and breathing out, again and again, I continued to feel the familiar movement of the breath until I had calmed down and I could see more clearly what needed to be done.*

The next step, tuning in, enables you to observe what is going on inside and to identify what you find difficult, tricky, or intolerable. It gives you an insight into yourself without having to react straightaway.

Friendly observation is the watchword

For a brief moment I focus on the inner chaos, the heart palpitations, and the hot fury that is flaring up in me like a local wildfire. I almost fell for it again. I almost gave in to that nearly uncontrollable urge to give short shrift to what I do not want to hear, feel, or experience. This has happened to me before, but this time I notice it. I am aware of the anger and my tendency to vent this anger. It makes a world of difference.

The backyard fence squeaks. The bike is thrown into the hedge, the back wheel dangling precariously. . . .

"Hey mom, guess what!? Our band's playing the school prom. Cool! I'm going to phone Jasper about that amp I told you about."

"That's great!" I am genuinely pleased for him and ask him if he would like something to eat . . . and what the doctor said.

"The doctor? No food, thanks, but what do you mean 'the doctor'?"

"Oh, nothing. I thought you were going to see the doctor this morning."

"Me?" he asks, sounding surprised. Meanwhile he digs his cell phone, which is almost an extension of his body, out of his pants pocket and calls Jasper. Although puzzled, I decide not to pursue the matter and to let it rest for now. Let's wait and see which way this wind blows. Tomorrow is another day.

The morning storm has died down. My son's teenage growing pains have started. I expect many more hurdles on the winding road from childhood to adulthood, and I am determined to bring my full attention to this journey. I know there will be difficult as well as beautiful moments ahead, and I want to be close—but not *too* close.

A time-out gives you the space to stop, while tuning in gives you the chance to connect with how you feel, how your body is reacting, and the role of your breathing. These are two important basic principles for mindful living with teenagers. Exercise 1 of the download can help you with this.

⊕ *Exercise 1 for Parents: Time Out, Tune In*

MINDFULNESS FOR PARENTS

Mindfulness does not solve problems, but it does give you the chance to be present in every moment, to bring your full attention to the present moment; to feel the sun on your skin and the wind in your hair. It makes you aware of the anxiety in your stomach when you do not know your child's whereabouts. It alerts you to the surprising maturity of your child that can shine through like an unexpected herald of spring. It connects you with the joy and misery, conflict and camaraderie you experience with your child—without your having to resolve anything or make it look better than it is, or without your having to give an immediate response

Most parents know how to go about raising their children. With the help of an instinctive and well-developed radar system, they can steer their children safely to adulthood. And most teenagers grow up without too many problems. Doubt, rebellion, rule breaking, experimenting with what is prohibited, as well as the many ordinary, everyday moments—we all know these are part of the process. But what do you do when things do not go according to plan? What if the influence you long thought you had suddenly loses its power?

It is not the end of the world if, every now and then, you cannot see the forest for the trees in your life with your teenagers. Nor does it matter if your children grossly exaggerate, gleefully rub your nose in your failings, or claim you are hopelessly old-fashioned. It gets tricky only when you and your teen are at risk of losing touch with each other, when you no longer know or feel what motivates each other, when your children consistently flout your rules, or when you may be drifting away from who you really are as you navigate challenging times.

Sooner or later we all face situations we would rather not be in. We can all suddenly find ourselves in dire straits for any number of reasons. At such moments you look for a stabilizer, for something to hold on to. Mindful attention is just such a stabilizer. It can be compared to a strong keel. In times of great emotional distress, a good keel will keep your boat well balanced, preventing it from "tipping over" at the first gust of wind and ensuring that in hurricane-force adolescent winds you can keep your hands on the controls—even if you cannot always determine the direction and the route and your influence will inevitably wane. By practicing mindful observation of your own personal weather conditions during periods of panic, stress, anxiety, or great concern, you can return to your center of calm. You will enjoy your most treasured moments in the good company of your mindful attention: moments of closeness, vulnerability, and openness.

Lucas has been skipping school a lot lately, and when he does attend, he is often sent out of class and given detention. It happened again this afternoon. He sends his mother a message: "I didn't do anything, but I've got detention again. This school's full of losers." She is ready for yet another barrage of "It wasn't my fault" and "They're so out of touch at school." When Lucas finally gets home, the radio is softly playing "Let Her Go" by Passenger, which was played at his grandmother's cremation. He stops in his tracks, and big tears start rolling down his face. He looks at his mother with an intensely sad expression in his eyes.

She, too, starts crying. With their arms wrapped tightly around each other, they drift on the strains of the music. When the song is over they continue to look at each other. "I love you, Mom," he says in a trembling voice. "I love you, too," she says warmly. Then he grabs his sports bag and swings it over his shoulder before giving her a big kiss and whispering softly: "We let her go, didn't we, Mom?"

Mindfulness is not a wonder drug or a miracle cure. Some people think it is the umpteenth form of navel gazing. Others believe that working on oneself only leads to egotism, to losing sight of others. Yet other people are afraid that learning to reflect on feeling fear or sadness could open up a can of worms. The opposite is true. Mindfulness is not therapy, either, but a daily practice through which to develop an awareness of the workings of your mind and the influence of your thoughts and feelings on your reactions. Mindfulness is not the same as positive thinking or wanting to take positive action. In fact, it is

not about thinking or doing at all. It is about "being"—
being present in the now.

MINDFULNESS MATTERS!

During the final class of a mindfulness course I give for
teenagers, Ronnie, age seventeen, slips a note into my hand
and whispers: "Read it at home, not now, or I'll be embar-
rassed!" In the note she says how much the classes have
helped her. "You may not realize it, but you've given me
something for the rest of my life."

The mother of an autistic boy tells me that the eight-
week parent training I teach has made her more aware of
the many good and wonderful moments with her son. In
the past, she tended to focus on everything that did not go
well. Now she gives herself the occasional break, as well as
more compassion. It enables her to tell herself occasionally:
"This is really hard. Go on, sit down, pour yourself a cup of
tea, and take some time for yourself instead of the family."

Breathe through This is based on the many Mindfulness
Matters! courses I have taught to children (ages four to
twelve), teenagers (ages thirteen to nineteen), educators
and mental-health professionals, and numerous parents
over the years. It is a sequel to the book *Sitting Still Like a
Frog*, which helps parents learn to hit the pause button every now and then. All the examples in this book are based
on true stories. Some of them come from the teenagers
and parents who have participated in my training programs

(their names have been changed to preserve anonymity), others are based on my own thirty-five years of experience as a mother.

COURAGE, COMPASSION, AND TRUST

When my children hit puberty, it caused the expected waves in our family. With the boys, things often just fell into place, but my daughter had her own unique take on what a teenager can and cannot do. She is the one who taught me most about myself. I learned just how much courage, compassion, and trust it takes to be a parent or a child in this digital age, in which our lives appear to be dominated by achievements, a glut of stimuli and choices, peer pressure, an urge to control, and an emphasis on results. This is why *Breathe through This* is made up of three parts: courage, compassion, and trust.

Courage is something you need as a parent in order to dispel the powerful myth that there is such a thing as perfect parenting. Likewise, you need courage to be the best possible role model to your children. Courage manifests as the guts it takes to face up to difficult situations and awkward feelings such as hurt, guilt or shame, and sadness. You also need courage to set boundaries. Courage gives you the chance to open up to what deep down in your heart you fear and hope you will never have to go through.

It takes compassion to connect with your own heart. Your heart is capable of giving and receiving tender and warm love, but it can just as easily shut off when it feels hurt. Compassion for yourself and others is characterized by the natural propensity to reduce suffering and pain and stimulate happiness. The challenge when raising children is to achieve a balance between your open mind (mindfulness) and your warm heart (heartfulness) so that you can combine intense feelings with judicious actions—especially when things are not going to plan.

Finally, trust is crucial for parents. Trust provides a fundamental sense of security and the belief that everything will be all right, even when present circumstances suggest otherwise. Trust is indispensable at times when we are forced to accept things we cannot control and have no choice but to sit back and wait. The tide will turn, as it always does; just be patient. A caterpillar always transforms into a butterfly; you can count on it—as long as you do not open the cocoon prematurely. You cannot influence the tides or, indeed, the weather or caterpillars—but you can have some control over your inner reactions, your attitude, and your behavior.

Your attitude determines the weight of the burden.

—*Eline Snel*

HOW TO USE THE AUDIO EXERCISES

This book includes links to downloads of two sets of mindfulness exercises—one for parents and one for teenagers (www.shambhala.com/breaththroughthis). These exercises can help you learn to live in the present moment, without judgment, without a preconceived objective, and without a particular result in mind. The more present-moment awareness you have, the less you miss. Presence leads to connection, which is of paramount importance, especially when living with teenagers. The exercises are flagged in the text with this download icon. Ⓓ You can do them while lounging at home on a couch or in an easy chair or while lying in bed. What matters is that you do them with the intention of genuinely wanting to experience them. You will learn to be fully present in everything you feel, think, or experience.

Each chapter also contains a few practical mindfulness tips. I have called them "Time-Out at Home," but you can do them anywhere, even while waiting in the supermarket checkout line. You do not need to sit on a little cushion. You can be mindful anytime, anyplace.

PART ONE

Courage

The word *courage* derives from the French *coeur* and the Latin *cor*, or heart. Courage enables you to face up to what, deep down in your heart, you fear and hope never to go through. Above all, it takes courage to take a mindful approach to parenting teenagers. Observing and examining your own reactions and feelings requires you to leave your comfort zone. And how do you feel about setting boundaries for your teenage child?

one

THE COURAGE TO OBSERVE
WITHOUT JUDGMENT

We have five senses through which we perceive the world around us. An additional, sixth, sense enables us to look inside ourselves. We can use it to determine how we feel, what we are thinking, and what physical sensations we have. The ability to reflect on and connect with our inner world every now and then is invaluable when raising children. The same is true for the ability to observe without judgment.

I see you for the very first time. I cannot stop looking at you. The sweet smell of warm milk, the feeling of skin on skin, and your healthy urge to live bypass my mind and penetrate all of my cells. My senses are alert and maternal before I even realize it. Focused on the now, they experience this moment pure and raw. I feel wonder. With your long eyelashes resting on your silky, soft cheeks, you breathe life in and out. Guileless, open, without judgment, and without expectations.

How come we are full of love and wonder when we look at newborn babies but far less so when we look at our adolescent children, let alone ourselves? Who or what inside us makes us want to interpret, explain, or judge ourselves and the teenagers around us? It is our thinking mind that views reality through a filter of old experiences or fixed patterns in our thoughts and emotions. This filter determines what reality we see and how we interpret, explain, and judge it. It also determines whether we like it or not.

This filter also shapes our response to a situation. Our perspective narrows and our capacity for nonjudgmental and mindful observation declines. From the time our children are very young, we tell them things like "Don't look at me like that," "Don't make a fool of yourself," "Pull yourself together," and "Stop being lazy." Emotions, interpretations, explanations, and expectations affect the way we perceive reality. What we think we see is often based more on what we think than what we actually see.

Anne walks in with a spring in her step and a large yellow shopping bag. She spent the afternoon shopping with my husband. "I got the most beautiful thing," she says, beaming. She unwraps a shiny, white, fake-leather jacket with a large collar made of some indeterminate furry material. She puts it on, holds the fake fur elegantly to her neck, and proudly twirls around the room. "What do you think, Mom?" she asks expectantly.

"I think it looks cheap," I say. "It's not you at all. You're not wearing that to school!"

As if stung by a wasp, she pulls off the jacket and throws it over a chair. "Why do you always spoil things?" she yells. "I wish I'd been born somewhere else, not here. You never think I look nice! You're always criticizing me."

I am about to protest, but before I have a chance to say that I think she always looks nice and, more important, that she is nice, she has already marched up to her room. She slams the door shut with the unspoken but clear message: Whatever you do, don't come upstairs, because I'm not opening the door!

ON AUTOPILOT

Most of the time, we are completely unaware of what we feel, think, say, or do, let alone the effect all of this has. We just blurt things out. Teenagers, parents, teachers—without realizing it, we often react as if we were on automatic pilot. Acting on autopilot is not bad in and of itself. In fact, it is quite useful and a lot less tiring to be on autopilot for a while. Pilots fly planes like this for hours on end until something major is about to happen, such as takeoff or landing, or something unexpected occurs, such as turbulence or a sudden calamity. This is when the autopilot system is switched off and the pilot takes over the controls again. Such a decision requires not only courage and good timing but also, above all, constant, calm monitoring of the changing circumstances during a flight. Living with teenagers is much the same.

Automatically, as if preprogrammed, my mind had wrapped and narrowed itself around the jacket; my mind descended on it to the exclusion of everything else. It is strange how our minds can keep circling around something we really like or dislike, so that we fail to notice everything else: the radiant look in her eyes, her proud bearing, and her need for affirmation of such a beautiful thing. I had not noticed any of it.

I sigh and kindly conclude that I got carried away again by the fully automatic reaction of instant judgment. The very thing I abhor. But there is no point in either rejecting or condemning myself for it. What is useful, however, is the realization that if I carry on reacting on autopilot, we are heading for a fight, which could result in alienation and distress.

By regularly observing myself and reflecting on what happens as soon as I air my views, I am more likely to stay out of the danger zone. The judgments keep coming—sometimes at lightning speed—but I don't voice them right away. I can simply notice them and let them pass. Slowly but surely I am beginning to have a better understanding of the workings of my mind. I don't always have to act on what I think, and what I think is not always true. My thoughts are nothing but opinions or interpretations. This reassures me and makes it easier for me to do things differently next time.

*When I take my daughter to her dance class a couple of hours
later, I apologize and say I should not have reacted like that
and that I did not mean it. "Sometimes I speak before I think."
I also tell her that I am pleased that she is so happy with
the jacket and that I hope she will get a lot of wear out of it.
Looking wise beyond her years, she accepts my apology and
mutters her forgiveness: "Oh, well, it just goes to show, parents
don't know it all."*

True. We don't know it all. And we don't need to either.

Mindful attention helps you identify your automatic reactions and judgments. Attention is like a spotlight. Every
thing picked out by the spotlight becomes visible, allowing
you to recognize your own response patterns, allowing you
to look, feel, and reflect on how you would like to respond
before you actually do so. Teaching your children how to
do the same will give them a skill that is worth its weight
in gold. If you allow yourself a moment of mindful attention between every situation and your reaction to it, you
create the necessary space for a conscious decision—free
from autopilot.

*At the parent training, a single mother is astounded by the
spontaneous change in her response patterns, simply by paying a little more attention to them. "Just a few weeks ago I'd*

often barge into the house, fuming with anger and complaining vociferously. 'Why can't you tidy the place up? What's so hard about that?' All I saw was the mess. And I'd comment on it, out of habit. Now I can see—beyond the mess—that they're doing their best to cook me a nice meal because I often come home tired. I enjoy it now and find it easier to accept that they don't always do it exactly the way I like it. And why should they do it just the way I like it? For the first time in years, I've told them how nice it smells when I walk in. It's really quite simple!"

The exercise Sitting Still Like a Frog helps you and your teenage children to recognize your automatic responses, to observe them and refrain from reacting right away. The frog sits still, breathes in and out, and observes—without judging and without wanting to change anything.

If you bring your attention to your breathing, you are present in this moment. Not in yesterday's moment, not in tomorrow's, but in the *now*. And that is what matters. Staying present with your breath does not change the situation as it is, only the way you experience it. It makes all the difference. Frequent practice helps you move out of your head and into your body. When your head is full of frustration and your patience is in short supply, try tapping into your breathing. Like an anchor, it stops you from drifting away. It keeps you grounded—here, in the present moment.

ⓧ *Exercise 2 for Parents: Sitting Still Like a Frog*

Taking time for yourself is a great challenge when you have growing children and family life is hectic. We are often far too busy to calm down and slow down. It takes courage to stop and take a break amid the hustle and bustle, as well as perseverance to keep training your attention, especially when you cannot see immediate results or it is not happening fast enough. Pulling at the grass does not make it grow faster; the same is true for the attention muscle.

TIME-OUT AT HOME
Observing without Judgment

Take a look at your teenage child at unguarded moments: sitting, sleeping, working at his or her computer, or chatting with friends. Look at your teen like you did when he or she was a baby—with that same warm gaze, without judgment. Act as if you were seeing your child for the first time. What do you see when you look with an open mind?

Why not look at yourself in the mirror every now and then with that same warm gaze and whisper, "I'm doing the best I can." And bear in mind that while there is no need to do things better, you could perhaps just do things differently.

What do you feel when you cast this warm gaze upon yourself? In life with teenage children, automatic response patterns are probably quite plentiful. Just think of your reactions to their putting off homework, messy rooms, dubious fashion choices, or excessive computer use. Notice your usual thought patterns about these. Stay with your automatic responses for a while. If you can summon the courage, you can decide to take the occasional left turn instead of your usual right. Observe the effect of this on yourself and your teenage child or children. Surprise yourself. And while you are at it, why not note which judgments keep rearing their head. How do you judge yourself as a parent? What do you think of your children, your partner, your ex? You can begin by accepting the judgments. Acknowledge them—without judging that too. If you were to draw up a top three, which judgments would top the chart?

Welcome your judgments and examine them. Accept them and smile at them as they enter your mind—but don't always express them. You see so much more when you look with an open mind.

two

THE COURAGE TO EXPLORE THE MIND-BODY CONNECTION

At a time when you and your teenage children are making your way through one of the most turbulent phases in the life of a family, it is absolutely indispensable to have a good connection between your body and your mind. With your mind connected to and in sync with your body and your heart, not only can you take better care of yourself and your children, but you can also help your children learn to look after themselves. It will stand them in good stead for the rest of their lives.

Your body provides a firm foundation for practicing mindful attention. Your body and your breath are always close.

Daniel is a tired father. During the intake interview prior to the parent training, he tells me that he travels the world as the manager of a large international manufacturer of aircraft components. He shares custody of his teenage daughters with his ex-wife. In a moment of openness he tells me about the many disagreements he's had with both his ex-wife and his two daughters about their upbringing. They say he is never there for them and that when he is around, he seems absent-minded and never really listens. He feels as though he and his daughters only ever talk in reproachful tones these days. And yet he adores them.

When he registers for the parent training, he is suffering from insomnia, dangerously high blood pressure, and seemingly unprovoked panic attacks. He is hoping to find some relief by starting meditation during the program. "Everybody's talking about it, so I'm sure I'll benefit from it."

We start the training. He is a little disappointed when we do the body scan, an exercise in connecting with the body. He thought he would dive straight in and achieve instant success. His body and mind are used to stress and are addicted to a fast pace. To begin with, he strains to be present in the here and now and present with his feet, a seemingly simple task. But he cannot do it. He cannot feel them. His mind has already returned to his head.

After the exercise, he gets up again with a sigh. When I ask him about his experience, he tells me the body scan was a failure. It was a disaster. Frustrated, he concludes that his busy foreign travel schedule is a lot easier for him than this journey around his own body.

"What do you mean when you say it was a failure?" I ask him. "What exactly went wrong?"

He remains a bit vague: "I just can't find any peace and

quiet. I keep thinking that I should concentrate better, should have paid more attention, that it's annoying that I just can't do it. I've faced bigger challenges than lying still on a mat. This is simple, right? Everybody can do it." He looks me straight in the eye, wanting me to confirm his notion that this exercise is incredibly easy and to acknowledge his powerlessness. I tell him that the difficulty of the exercise lies in its simplicity. It is like learning to walk; it looks deceptively simple, but the first time you try, it is pretty hard. I ask him if he is prepared to reflect on his idea that he cannot do it. What is the real issue here? He is quiet for a moment, nods, and eventually tells me: "I was always taught that there is no such thing as 'can't do,' that it equals 'won't do.' 'Where there's a will, there's a way,' my father used to say. I kept hearing this phrase during the exercise." He raises his hands and drops his head into them—a desperate gesture. "It's all I know."

Sad eyes reflect an old, unhealed wound. It is quiet in the room, but his words still resonate. The whole group has been listening with open, warm attention— and with recognition, too. Unspoken understanding ripples gently through the room. We all feel it. Here is something important, something fundamental. Softly, I tell him he is doing fine. He does not have to do better or try harder. He looks surprised. In the group we talk about how the body scan is not about trying to feel something you do not feel (yet) or changing what you do experience. Nor is it about relaxing or trying incredibly hard. It is just *about gradually getting used to directing your attention to all parts of your body.*

In the weeks that follow, Daniel first notices what to him feels like terrifying tension, the restlessness in his body, and the excessive pace at which he moves through life. From an early age he has been intent on achieving the best results in school, on performing well in sports, and on continuing to get ahead at work. He was pushed by his ambitious parents, by teachers who told him he could do much better, and by coaches at work who encouraged him to aim higher and meet his targets. And now his marriage had ended because he was pushing himself and his children.

It takes courage to find your way back to basics, to feel compassion for your body when it works too hard and is under constant pressure. It takes both guts and love to walk away from old, dead-end patterns that make you neglect your body until it is worn out and starts showing unhealthy symptoms.

As he practices the body scan more and more often, Daniel begins to experience moments of peace. He still struggles to connect with many parts of his body—they remain unknown territory for him—but he can accept that. The experience of not having to achieve is new to him: strange, but fascinating at the same time.

Mindful awareness not only brings pleasant things to light but also illuminates those things that you may have turned a blind eye to in the past.

Over the next few weeks Daniel is to direct his attention to moments when he feels tension and stress bubble up in his body, not to ignore his physical symptoms but to give them his full attention. I also ask him to reflect on all of those moments when, as soon as he relaxes, he starts putting pressure on himself again—automatically, without realizing it.

Amazed by it all, he experiences a condition previously unknown to him: inner peace, a kind of profound satisfaction, prompting him to make different choices and to feel happier in his life. His daughters notice it too: "You'll keep on meditating, won't you, Dad? When you're doing well, we do better too."

The body scan helps both teenagers and parents to move out of the head and into the body. Unless you connect with the body, you cannot really *feel* how you are doing—you can only *think* about how you are doing. There is a fundamental difference. You will notice the difference when you are doing the body scan. You can do it with the help of the audio download or without it, in the middle of the day, while waiting at the supermarket checkout, or anywhere. How do your feet, your legs, and the rest of your body feel at this moment? And what do you need to calm down?

OUT OF YOUR HEAD AND INTO YOUR BODY

Teenagers, too, have trouble experiencing, examining, and accepting feelings in their body. While the outside is subjected to merciless scrutiny, the inside is often neglected.

Relentlessly and with the precision of an experienced biologist in search of unknown species, my daughter scans her appearance for flaws before, during, and after school. "Do you expect me to go to school with this bird's nest hair? And as for the boots, I'm not wearing them anymore. People look at me like I'm weird when I have those things on." I stare at her in shock. There is nothing wrong with those brand-new boots, and her hair looks great too. But convinced she "looks like a mess," she stays locked in the bathroom for another thirty minutes.

Many people think about their body rather than *feel* it. Both parents and teenagers have this notion that their body is like a collection of car parts they can replace as they see fit or take to the garage for respraying or repairing. But of course your body is a lot more than that.

Whether or not you are present in your body, all of your body's components work closely together, communicate with one another, and emit signals when things are too much, too little, or just right. And you live among this wonderfully cooperative system, which consists of so much more than just a head. For a closer look at this unique collaboration, I recommend the following exercises. You can do them with your teenage child or with someone else.

TIME-OUT AT HOME
In Touch with Your Body

Take a pen, a pencil, or some other small object close at hand. Sit down on the couch and put the object about three or four feet away from you on the floor. Then pick it up in slow motion, becoming aware of all the different parts of the body involved in this action. Do you pick up the object using only your hand or are other parts of the body involved too? What about your tongue, your toes, or your back? Are there any parts of the body not involved in this action? Which are they? Are they really not involved, or did you just not notice? As you repeat the exercise, you will discover more and more about the most unique collaborative effort imaginable.

For the next exercise you need to stand facing another person. Put your palms together and try to push each other over, using only your hands, not the muscles in your arms, legs, buttocks, or back. What happens when you use only one part of the whole? Can you apply pressure?

Next bring in your arms. See what happens when you use two parts of your body to fulfill a task. And now use your whole body. What happens when all the parts of your body cooperate? And who is actually observing this cooperation?

Try to connect with your body three times a day. Start things off just before you get up. How does your body feel at this moment in time? Still tired? Well rested? Is there any soreness? Do you have any other sensations? Choose two additional moments, perhaps while you are talking to others. What is your body trying to tell you when you are having a difficult conversation? Or at the end of the workday?

Teenagers often underestimate their body's signals. They do not know their limits. In fact, they often do not even know what this expression means. They keep going, however many red lights are flashing. Dangers are rationalized away: "Everyone's doing it. You used to do it too, right?" Experiments can result in dangerous addictions.

But adults, too, have a tendency to ignore alarm signals and to keep going. We do not take the time to eat or go to the bathroom. We deny our symptoms: "Me, tired? Not at all!" And we rationalize by saying: "Surely I can't let my colleagues . . . children . . . spouse down?"

Our body listens to us—not the other way around. We push it, drag it up and down the stairs, and force it into our cars or onto public transportation or onto our bikes. We sit at our computers with hunched shoulders, and we go on vacation feeling stressed. As long as the body does not complain and remains strong and well rested, we tend not to worry too much. But what happens when stress, pain, or uncomfortable feelings crop up?

Mindfulness teaches you to reinhabit your body and to examine, feel, and experience everything under your skin, just as it is. As soon as you know how your body is feeling, you can give it what it needs. With a couple of minutes of mindful attention, you take a bit of time to look after yourself and not just others.

three

THE COURAGE TO
ADMIT YOUR FEELINGS

To feel your breath, your body, and your emotions again, you need an open mind and a warm heart. Knowing that you have them is one thing, but allowing yourself to truly experience them is another. Like thoughts, feelings are a direct and often automatic response to what you are experiencing or imagining. In a family with children going through puberty, strong emotions can cause turmoil for both parents and children. Fear and insecurity, as well as feelings of guilt or shame, are more common emotions for parents during this period than when the children were little.

You can connect with your feelings by opening up to them instead of suppressing or denying them. The rough edges of disappointment, fear, rejection, sadness, or anger take possession of your body without warning and often in a split second. When you get carried away by them, it may seem as if you *are* your feelings.

You can feel them in the pit of your stomach, close to your heart, or in the muscles of your neck, shoulders, or jaw.

Giving time and attention to these feelings allows you the option to respond differently to them than you are used to doing. If you react to them with mindful awareness, you will begin to understand cause and effect. You will attain wisdom.

We are sitting on the couch, watching an incredibly beautiful film.

"This is nice, isn't it, Mom?" my daughter says.

My heart is close to bursting. I'm thinking, "If only it could be like this forever."

But, as we all know, life is changeable, unpredictable, and certainly not in our control. Nothing stays the same. Before long, this becomes all too clear

Our fifteen-year-old son is smoking pot. I discover it by accident when, after calling him for dinner for the umpteenth time, I enter his room without knocking. He nervously sticks something inside an empty can of Coke, while a guilty flush steals across his stubbly cheeks. Every parent's nightmare surges through my body like lightning.

"What are you doing?" I say more sharply than intended.

After some initial spluttering, he comes out with it, his eyes lowered. He has been smoking cigarettes for a while, but now he is smoking dope too. It turns out he has been doing it for some time. I had a sneaking suspicion, and had even asked

him about it, but he always said: "Oh no, of course not. I wouldn't do a thing like that!"

I feel angry and betrayed. How can he be so stupid? I also feel naive and gullible. I thought we had an agreement. . . . We had promised to pay for his driving lessons if he stayed away from dope until he was eighteen.

TO FEEL OR NOT TO FEEL

Both teenagers and parents frequently deploy the following three mechanisms to deal with or avoid uncomfortable or difficult feelings:

Get carried away by them
Suppress them
Deny them

You cannot prevent unpleasant feelings—neither your own nor your child's. But you can make sure you do not shut yourself off from them. Each and every feeling is important to our human experience. At times we are all sad, deeply moved, or overwhelmed by strong emotions. It happens to everyone, including you and your children. Being bullied, excluded, or humiliated is terrible, whereas it is wonderful to receive a compliment, feel relief, or fall in love for the first time. All of these pleasant and unpleasant feelings present you with the same choice: Do I shut myself off from them or open up to them?

The moment I realize my son is smoking dope, I choose to open up to the maelstrom of feelings this evokes. I decide to observe them as if from behind a waterfall. What exactly am I feeling? And where in my body are those feelings located? I feel the fear of his impending addiction like electric waves in my stomach. The shock of the discovery is evident in my breath, which I keep holding, while I register the anger at his furtive behavior in the tightening of my muscles. Then, funnily enough, my anger makes way for a brainstorm. Surely I never expected him to say, all bright and breezy: "All right, Mom, I'm going to light up another joint, if it's okay with you."

The decision not to immediately blow my top gives me the time to think and to reconnect with my mind and my heart. I decide that I will talk with him—not now but when the worst of the storm is over and the air is clear again on both sides.

Opening up to difficult feelings requires courage. You need to have the guts to face up to what scares you when you are more inclined to turn away. But if you suppress or ignore your feelings or allow yourself to be drawn into their vortex, you deprive yourself of the opportunity to feel just how bad it is. Or how wonderful. Opening up to your emotions, instead of shutting yourself off from them, helps you to look after yourself. As you learn to do so, you can examine what you need in the situation and ask yourself what might really help you now.

The following evening my son and I have a conversation. His head is clear again, and the fire of my anger has been quenched. I want to hear the whole story. He tells me about his group of friends.

"They all smoke dope. You know, when we're hanging out. It's relaxing to have nothing on your mind."

In answer to my question about when and how often he does it, he says rather casually: "Oh, sometimes during the week, but usually just on the weekend—when we're chilling. It's easy to get hold of on the streets near school, and Jasper always has money, so he shares his joints with me. Really nice of him."

I ask him gently whether he has thought about the consequences of drug use. He laughs a little uneasily and says: "Nah . . . I just do it. Nobody gives it a second thought. Everybody just does it."

When I press him about what smoking a joint does for him, he answers: "I finally get to relax. It calms my mind like nothing else. And we usually laugh a lot too. Like someone will get started laughing for no reason. It's hilarious!"

I nod and look at him intently. It is quiet. We are connecting. Then I ask him to listen to me, and I tell him everything I know about the different classes of drugs, which is quite a lot.

Parents of teenage children might want to look into drugs and their effects so they know more than their kids do.

He is listening. His young eyes look at me and express their relief: "She has looked into this. She thinks it is important." But when I ask him to stop smoking dope, a shadow crosses his face. His face conveys doubt, fear, and insecurity.

"How am I supposed to stop?" he asks irritably. "They'll laugh at me. I know it. They'll think I'm one of those losers who does exactly what his parents tell him to."

"Well," I say, "I can see where you're coming from, and there is that risk. But it's nothing compared with the risks of smoking pot."

For the first time, those risks are now becoming painfully clear to him. He grows angry, uneasy at the thought of having to do something because of unforeseeable risks. He faces some difficult decisions, and he will have to take responsibility for his own life: Do I want to stop? What am I prepared to give up? And what will take its place?

Now I get to the crux of the matter: "Smoking dope is off-limits. You're not allowed to do it at home or any other place. Nowhere and with no one." My message is clear. I have sympathy for his experiment, his need to try this, but that is as far as it goes. It is time for some clear rules.

I have treated him with respect, but I have given a boundary, too, and he is aware of it. His anger subsides. It is making way for something else. The knowledge that he no longer has to sneak around calms him. It comforts him, too: my parents are here for me, although they do not approve of everything I do.

All you need to do when you are caught in such a maelstrom of feelings is to notice the process and feel and admit those feelings. Talking candidly and listening with open ears and an open heart are essential to every relationship. You may feel that you are flitting dangerously close to the abyss at times, but living with teenagers calls for respect for their feelings, candid communication, and clear boundaries. And all of this requires courage.

The drug taking does not stop overnight. Nor do our conversations. His fear of being the only one to stop and my suspicion that he is still smoking continue to simmer, like a soup that needs time to develop its flavors. Simply telling him to stop would be pointless, I realize; his awareness needs to be raised too.

He ends up talking to someone in the neighborhood who knows a lot about addiction. It helps him find a position that accommodates both his own perspective and our house rules. It gives him the guts to quit.

And I give myself time to pay attention to the changing weather conditions inside myself. I notice that the feelings themselves do not last all that long, ranging from just a few seconds to a couple of minutes. The disaster scenarios in my head tend to cause the distress, but there is no real cause for concern now that he has quit.

By not reacting to unpleasant feelings right away, you train yourself in the art of equanimity. Take the time to notice various impulses and to let them go again. This way you develop not only the courage to feel feelings and emotions but also the strength to bear them without screaming, complaining, or expressing your misery verbally. This is not a case of suppressing your irritation or anger but of letting the pulsating energy move through you while you observe the feelings kindly, patiently, with the bravery of a warrior. You admit them and note how big, heavy, or light they are and what impact they have on your mood and your behavior. You can leave them be, if they are there, for as long as they are there. Feel them, unpolished and raw as they are—perhaps they are even extremely painful. Advance with caution, as if approaching a deer at the edge of the forest that could suddenly dart away.

YOU'RE NEVER TOO YOUNG TO LEARN

Feelings themselves rarely cause problems. After all, they are just feelings. The problems tend to arise as a result of what we think about the feelings and the many strategies we devise for not having to feel them. This tends to start early in childhood. Minor incidents (your mother is angry because you dropped something), terrible memories (your father leaves suddenly, never to return), feelings of rejection ("Don't be childish")—all of them are stored in our young subconscious like absolute truths and projected onto ourselves: "I am bad; nobody loves me."

Children rarely question their parents' behavior. After all, they are your parents; they know what's what. And so the children question themselves. "It must be my fault." These erroneous conclusions prompt survival strategies that we carry over into adulthood. We are afraid to say no, we work too hard, or we take care only of other people's needs while neglecting our own. We can keep going like this for a long time, until it catches up with us and causes harm both to us and to our children.

We were all children once, so we all, to a greater or lesser degree, developed survival strategies and attendant behavioral patterns. There was a time when these things offered adequate protection against unpleasant feelings and helped us to stand our ground, to survive. In our adult lives, however, we no longer need these strategies. We are capable of supporting and comforting ourselves. Teenagers have yet to discover this. And they have to discover it through trial and error. You are the one to teach them to open up to both unpleasant and pleasant feelings. Just be prepared for them to protest: "Mom, Dad, shut up, will you?!"

Try stepping into your child's shoes. What uncomfortable thoughts and feelings do you remember from your own adolescence? How did you handle them? What pleasant feelings do you remember from your childhood? What do you wish your parents had done? Do you ever ask your children what they would like you to do or to give them so that they can boost their self-confidence?

(⊥) *Exercise 4 for Parents: Handling Difficult Feelings*

MELTING THE ICE

Thomas, age sixteen, is one of a group of eight young people from a special-needs school where my daughter and I do mindfulness coaching. He is a quiet, introverted young man who often feels a bit down. He is extremely sensitive but does not show that he is. He self-harms occasionally "just to feel something."

Marianne, who is fifteen, has another issue. She is head over heels in love, but earlier this week she saw her boyfriend kissing someone else. It makes her angry and sad at the same time. She does not know what to do with these feelings, but she is making things hard on other students by calling them names and belittling and bullying them. "Don't mess with me" is what she seems to be saying. Talking about feelings is one thing, but genuinely feeling them is quite another, which the students discover while doing the following exercise.

"Will you hold out your hand, please?" As I place an ice cube in each of the students' hands, I ask them to note their initial reaction. Thomas says he wants to drop the ice on the floor right away. It is too painful. But then he clenches his jaw and holds

his wrist with his other hand as if clutching a hot steel frying pan containing a dangerous substance. He does not flinch but hops from foot to foot while his muscles become tense. Marianne is running around in circles, yelling all sorts of things: "Oh no, cold, cold, cold! What a stupid exercise! Do you have any idea how much this hurts? Want me to show you?"

Then I ask the group to stop moving and shouting, to focus on their breathing, and to admit and observe all the thoughts and feelings they are having. During the discussion afterward they tell me they noticed a range of feelings: shock, pain, and fear. Likewise, they were acutely aware of the physical sensations: cold and wet. "Where the ice cube lies you feel nothing at first or just a slight burning sensation."

What strikes me is that everybody's initial reaction is the same: resistance, not wanting to feel it. But with the courage of a regiment of warriors, they persevered, only to notice the ice melting— just like strong feelings: they too disappear like snow in summer.

They never realized this until now. If you admit something you prefer to get rid of, you will, paradoxically, find that even the most intense feelings will melt. But you will have that experience only if you have the courage to feel your feelings.

TIME-OUT AT HOME
An Exercise in Noticing

Perhaps there is a feeling you tend to suppress, ignore, or numb. Let's see if you can start by simply noticing it today.

Again, approach it like you would a deer: with caution and respect. Do not rush it. What kind of feeling is it? What effect does it have on your body? What do you do with what you suppress, ignore, or numb? What happens when you accept it into the warmth of your heart?

Also, notice a good feeling that you are having today. What prompted it? Where in your body do you feel it? For how long do you feel it? What is happening to your face and to your heart when you feel it? What are your thoughts about it? What happens when you allow this feeling into your heart?

Make time when your child wants to talk to you about his or her feelings. Listen with an open mind and a warm heart without wanting to resolve things right away, saying there is no need for the child to feel that way, or making light of the problem.

If your teenage child does not want to discuss his or her feelings with you, you could ask if there is anyone the child ever shares feelings with a friend for instance, or someone online. Genuine interest and sincere concern count for a lot more with your teenager than speeches do.

four

THE COURAGE TO
FACE UP TO STRESS

From the moment your children were born until now you will have had your heart in your throat many times and found yourself having to adjust your ideas about what successful parenting looks like. We want to do well, but there are so many things that can go unexpectedly wrong: divorce, sudden illness, bullying, or months of disturbed nights because your teenage child is no longer coming home on time.

Raising children can be very stressful. But what is stress? What causes it? Is stress the same as tension, or is it something else? Why does one parent suffer from stress while the other, in exactly the same situation, simply says: "Relax, it'll be fine." Why does one teenager sail through exams while another does not? It has to do with the fact that it is not the situation itself that causes the stress, but our thoughts about it.

STRESS IS AN UNAVOIDABLE PART OF PARENTING

There are internal sources of tension and stress for parents, such as perfectionism and feelings of insecurity, as well as external ones, such as exams, sporting achievements, life-style changes, or arguments with an ex. They make us feel threatened in certain situations (real or imagined), and we generally respond to threats by fighting, fleeing, or freezing.

A bit of tension can be fun and even healthy. Just before a big party you are organizing, or prior to a presentation, the adrenaline gives you what you need to achieve great things. It sharpens your senses so that you can concentrate and respond adequately to everything that arises.

Your body is perfectly capable of dealing with short-term tension, but when you are exposed to situations that undermine your resilience and your sense of well-being for longer periods of time, the result is stress. And long-term stress can lead to numerous symptoms: physical (headache, neck pain, pain in the shoulders or other parts of the body), mental (trouble concentrating, anxiety, or fear of failure), and/or emotional (weepiness, irritability, short-temperedness). Stress can cause serious illness, burnout, or depression.

Stress is a temporary but unavoidable part of raising children. Stress symptoms increase in parents and teenage children alike when they feel their control over a situation slipping. This is particularly common when faced with exams, major sporting events, or heavy work pressure. You never know how things will pan out (which is not to say we do know in other situations). When you are present with your thoughts and feelings about stress, you will notice that the sensations are coupled with an innate ability to observe and to breathe with that stress. You can observe it instead of getting carried away by it or ignoring it. As a result, your futile attempts at stopping or fighting your stress will decrease, while your ability to really be there for yourself increases. Exercise 5 on the download, A Good Start to the Day, can help you with this.

⊕ *Exercise 5 for Parents: A Good Start to the Day*

UNDERSTANDING THE WORKINGS OF YOUR MIND

Parents' minds are often in overdrive. And we tend to think it is our teenage children's behavior that makes us angry or causes us stress, but this is a misconception. It is not so much the behavior itself but our thoughts about it that cause the tension.

Dorothy is livid when her son comes home two hours later than agreed. "It's really getting me down," she says to me. "I don't know what to do to make him come home on time. Nothing seems to work. He just doesn't listen."

When I ask her what thought is making her feel depressed, she replies it is her son who is making her feel she can no longer handle things. After I press her on the issue and repeat my question, she suddenly realizes that she often thinks, "My children don't respect me." This is it. This one negative thought is causing her depressive feelings, not her teenage son's behavior. A closer look at thoughts triggered by feelings of tension or stress reveals that there are potentially plenty of other ways to think about the same situation, for example:

This is typical teenage behavior.
Oh, well, I did the same when I was that age.
I do not demand respect.
They are just testing me now that their father no
    longer lives at home.
Let me see how to demand respect.
Nobody can anger me or stress me out except me.

The realization that we can influence our thoughts has a strangely calming effect. But to do so you have to get to know, identify, and acknowledge them first. Thoughts are just thoughts. Not facts but what your mind thinks about the facts. Isn't that remarkable? You can learn to control, identify, acknowledge, and even question the veracity of thoughts. It all starts with observation. Watch your mind for a while—perhaps while doing the dishes, right before a sports activity, driving, or while stuck in traffic—and you will notice all kinds of thoughts, such as the following:

Thoughts about yourself: If only I . . .

Thoughts about someone else: He would do a lot
    better if he tried a bit harder.

Doubtful thoughts: Am I giving my child enough
    attention? Or perhaps too much?

Worried thoughts: What if he . . . ?

Untrue thoughts: I'll never manage to . . .

Children, too, are beset with hundreds of doubts and fears: about their social circle, about school or the situation at home, about the changes they are going through. Often the parents' stress also gets passed on to the child. In many cases, parents are only echoing the behavior and continuing the stressors that were a part of their own childhood.

Twelfth grader Mascha comes home from school looking tired and pale. She has been sleeping badly for some time now. Her perfectionism—and that of her parents, who were pushed to be at the top of their class by their own parents—means that she often raises the bar too high for herself. She goes to extreme lengths to succeed: exam training, homework help, review exercises, quizzes, hours of after-school study; you name it. Failure is unheard of in her family.

When I ask her in a friendly way whether there is any point in studying until late at night, only to get up really early to go through everything again, she answers irritably: "Yes, of course there is! Don't tell me there's not! If I don't, I can forget about my education. I want to be a doctor, and that won't just happen." Her lips purse and her body tenses. She has had no time off for months.

Fear of failure and wanting to stay in control prompt Mascha either to study relentlessly or to escape (by eating chocolate and bags of chips). You may be familiar with these responses to stress. It is not the exam itself but the eternal doubts. How do you know something is good enough? You may well forget tomorrow what you learned today. And so the stress builds and builds.

Our mind produces some three thousand thoughts per waking hour. This amounts to an average of fifty-two per minute, or nearly one every second. That's a lot. Before you know it, you get swept along by them, and your mind will be on something other than what you were working on. And . . . do you believe everything you think? What are you to do with all of these thoughts?

As part of the Mindfulness Matters! training program in schools and the parent-training sessions, we explore the workings of our mind to get used to the idea that while we have thoughts, we are not those thoughts. If we were, we would not be able to observe them. In the following training exercise, we start with a kind of game, which you can also do at home.

STOP YOUR THOUGHTS FOR ONE MINUTE

The young people in the group are given the task to stop thinking—and they are absolutely not to think about a bunch of yellow bananas. "Easy!" Joe comments. Starting now. A minute later I see tense faces. They try their hardest but cannot do it. I ask them what they noticed during this one minute?

The children explain that they were unable to suppress the thought of yellow bananas. When you try to force your mind in a certain direction, you usually achieve the exact opposite. Not only is it hard to suppress all thought of bananas when you want to, but as soon as you give free rein to your thoughts, yellow bananas crop up far more often than if you never tried not to think of them. And if this is true for neutral thoughts, you can imagine what happens with troubling thoughts.

KNOWING AND STEERING YOUR MIND

As soon as you get to know your mind better, you will be more attuned to its stories, judgments, and interpretations and its litany of "I must do this and I must do that." You will also recognize just how often your thoughts are preoccupied with either the past or the future. "Ah, I'm worrying right now" or "I'm worried about something I'm doing four weeks from now" or "If only things were still . . ."

Thoughts are restless, always in search of stimuli. They

are all over the place, reacting impulsively and going off on tangents. By following them for a while, you will get to know them and, providing you do not pursue every "what if" or "what next," even calm them down. You will also find it easier to make decisions: "Shall I pursue this or say, 'No, not now'?"

Cultivating mindful awareness and a clear mind can help you break from unhelpful thoughts and reaction patterns. Entering into a different relationship with your thoughts makes you less dependent on their content, enabling you to see that awareness and having thoughts are two entirely different matters. This will prompt some remarkable discoveries: you have thoughts, but you are not those thoughts. You cannot stop thoughts, but you can stop listening to them all the time.

A mind at rest is in a much better position to learn and memorize things than a stressed out mind. When you are less in the grip of panic reactions, you can remain the captain of your own fate and make other, more deliberate and beneficial choices. When a wave of emotion threatens to wash you away, it always helps to return to the breath.

You cannot stop the waves in life, but you can learn to surf on them. Needless to say, this is not always easy. Surfing is a difficult sport. But as you practice, you learn how to be fully present with the wave that is coming at you now. You learn to harness its force and incredible energy so you can stay upright. So you are riding the wave instead of drowning. What a great sensation!

Stress and tension are temporary but unavoidable. You cannot control the situations that give rise to them, but you can control the way you respond to them. And this is comforting to know.

If you find yourself lying awake at night worrying about everything that needs to be done or that is not going well in your view, there are two things you can do: notice that you are worrying, and move out of your head and into your body. Exercise 6 on the download, The Conveyor Belt of Worries, can help you do this.

⊕ *Exercise 6 for Parents: The Conveyor Belt of Worries*

TIME-OUT AT HOME
An Exercise in Recognition

Recognizing Different Kinds of Thoughts

As soon as you wake up in the morning, you can start watching the active stream of thoughts in your mind. What are you thinking of?

Yourself or others?
The past or the future?

Everything that needs to be done?
Worries?
Things you did not do well?
Something else?

Check how often your thoughts return to the same subject. For example:

The past
Worries about the future
Your children
Your job
Your partner

An Exercise to Do While Worrying

While you are worrying, if you shift your attention from your head to the movement of your breath in your belly, you will learn that while you cannot stop your thoughts, you can stop listening to them. This will calm your mind, allowing you to deal with the things you want to deal with instead of the persistent, intruding thoughts.

The defining feature of anxious thoughts is that they keep coming back, going around and around in circles without ever really landing on a solution. In fact, worrying never provides a solution. Clear thinking does, but you can think clearly only when your mind has calmed down.

The thirteenth-century Persian poet Rumi wrote a poem on the subject, "The Guest House," a portion of which follows:

Darling, the body is a guest house;
every morning someone new arrives.
Don't say, "O, another weight around my neck!"
or your guest will fly back to nothingness.
Whatever enters your heart is a guest
from the invisible world: entertain it well.
   [...]
If a sorrowful thought stands in the way,
it is also preparing the way for joy.
It furiously sweeps your house clean,
in order that some new joy may appear from the
      Source.
It scatters the withered leaves from the bough of the
      heart,
in order that fresh green leaves might grow.
It uproots the odd joy so that
a new joy may enter from Beyond.
   [...]
Whenever sorrow comes again,
meet it with smiles and laughter,
saying "O my Creator, save me from its harm,
and do not deprive me of its good.

Lord, remind me to be thankful,
let me feel no regret if its benefit passes away."

See if you can watch your thoughts or feelings with respect. Get to know them, like guests in a guesthouse run by you. One guest will be a lot nicer than another, but still . . . they all arrive looking for shelter. Every guest is important and teaches you something about yourself, especially those guests you dislike.

five

THE COURAGE TO SET BOUNDARIES

Adolescence is crunch time when it comes to setting boundaries. Weak points or thin skin can cause undue stress or irritation in your relationship with your teenage children. From the age of two or three, children start testing ways of getting what they want. If you have a habit of giving in just to stop the whining, you teach your child that nagging, yelling, and manipulating are effective. The child will then start to hone its strategy. Ten years down the line your teen will deploy the same weapons to receive a bigger allowance or permission to smoke or to stay out as long as the she or he wants.

Children will continue to use this strategy to get what they want for as long as it works. But there is something else going on as well. When children have no firm foundation to fall back on, they become insecure and fearful. Because every time a child gets the better of his or her parent, that parent shows that he or she is not firm enough. The child will go further and further until he or she encounters resistances and realizes: Ah, this is how far I can go. This is the limit. Here's where I hit a wall.

"Do you think I'm strict?" I ask my nearly thirteen-year-old daughter, Anne, while we are out grocery shopping. I have just told her that one bag of potato chips a week is more than enough.

"Strict?" Her smiling eyes tell me something I have suspected for a while. She kindly explains that if she wants something, she will go on and on about it because in the end I usually give in. I look at her, stunned.

Okay, so that's how it works. Thank you, my daughter, for identifying my weak spot. From now on I will give it my full attention. I will keep working on it until I can say: Here's where I draw the line. No means no. I am through with the nagging and the giving in.

My daughter's incisive observation and her strong character have put me on the alert. I must act while I can; in a year or two it will be too late. Once children hit fourteen, fifteen, there is little you can do as a parent. She is already growing up too fast. I see it happening, unable to stop or influence it. My crash course starts later the same day. Clearly there is no time to lose.

PUTTING UP WITH THE NAGGING

A moment of intense enjoyment: it is the weekend, the house is full of young people, and there is homemade soup and freshly baked French bread on the table. Life is good. The boys are home with their girlfriends and Anne is flitting around the place. Occasionally, and much to her brothers' horror, she jumps between the couples on the couch.

"Hey, Anne, what do you think you're doing?" they yell.

Looking triumphant, she smiles her sweetest smile and says, "Can I squeeze in? Please?"

"Just this once. And then you'll leave us alone, okay?"

She nods meekly and wriggles her bottom to make more space for herself. After our meal the boys and their girlfriends all go off to do their own thing, while Anne locks herself in the bathroom for an hour. With big black panda eyes, hastily applied blusher on her cheeks, and a sweater that appears to have shrunk in the wash, she comes hurtling down the stairs. I look at her in shock and think, "You look terrible," but I keep my mouth shut.

"Mom, what time do I have to be home tonight? Everyone else can stay out till one."

"Until one?" I say, "No way! You're thirteen years old! I want you home by eleven."

"Eleven? Have you been living under a rock, or what? No-body, and I mean nobody, has to be home that early. Most parents don't even specify the time. Lily gets to decide herself, and so does Caroline. Everybody, in fact. It's not a problem. Come on, give me a break! I'm coming home at one! Like it or lump it."

The pressure is stepped up. The great nagging has begun. I can feel my shoulder muscles twitching. I do not want this. I thought we had been through this. I thought I had made myself clear on this point. I do not want any whining this evening. Not now! We were having such a nice time.

I notice minor tremors of fear on my internal Richter scale. Something is pushing me into a corner where I feel vulnerable and unable to respond the way I would like to. Cloudy thoughts and waves of adrenaline keep getting in the way.

What am I supposed to do if she rejects me as a mother because I am too strict? What if she ignores me and I lose control? Or what if she stops coming home altogether and moves out, as she is always threatening to do? My mind is spinning. It is an old battle, and I expect to bear the scars for a long time to come. While she nags and nags, the pressure inside me mounts like it does inside a pressure cooker with a closed safety valve. No . . . hold it right there! I cannot stand it anymore.

I ask her to stop, but she carries on, raging about my ridiculous response and saying what a stupid mother I am, before snatching the front door key off the table and preparing to leave. Wearing my jacket.

"I'm leaving," she says, and heads for the door.

Why is she so darn difficult? Why can't she just do as I ask for a change? Nothing is ever easy with her. The constant criticism. It is exasperating. But most exasperating of all is my own vulnerability. My doubts. My inability just to say, "No, *this is where I draw the line!" What is so hard about that? It has never been an issue at work, or with the boys. But with her . . . She goes straight for the jugular. Alarm bells are going off in my head. Action is needed now.*

I grab her by the jacket and force her to look me straight in the eye. My voice is clear, calm, and friendly. There is no room for negotiation about her curfew. "Anne, it's eleven o'clock and that's it. Not a second later!"

"Okay, whatever," she snaps. "It'll be your fault if they all laugh at me." She walks off in a huff.

I am exhausted. And I know this is just the beginning.

RESTORING THE FOUNDATIONS

Something deep inside me is crying. At once gently and painfully, it points me in the direction of a long-hidden and vulnerable spot in my foundation. I feel miserable. It is difficult to approach, but I know from experience that there is something else behind this feeling: the space to stand up for my own interests. I direct my attention to the breath and note its ever-changing movements. It imbues me with calm and confidence: the breath is always present.

Then I proceed to the very palpable and injured spot in my inner world. Close to my heart.

What is there? What do I feel there? Cautiously, I move closer and switch on the light. It illuminates all of those previously

dark places. Now I can see and feel them. There is pain, sad-
ness. An incredible loneliness and fear of rejection come to
light. With the courage of an intrepid explorer, I stay with it.
Images emerge. My "no" was not accepted. My opposition was
irrevocably punished. There was no room for negotiation or
a personal opinion. Anne did as she pleased. Gently, I admit
the injured feelings. I address them lovingly with the following
words: "It's okay." I am present and release the steam that has
been building for far too long. The valve is open now. A fresh
wind blows through my spirits.

So this is what was bothering me! I had to go to the
place where my opinion was stifled, my autonomy was
curtailed, and my fear of rejection or disappointing others
originated. My heart's warm embrace creates space, leaving
me free to negotiate more with my daughter, to put up
with the nagging; to clearly draw the line and, above all,
not to lose my sense of humor. I keep a close eye on her.
Adjust some things, suspend some rules if necessary. And
I demand respect, as much respect as I show her. I do it
out of love, trust, responsibility, and care—no longer out
of fear.

I am grateful for the mirror my daughter kept holding
up to me, enabling me to feel the resistance. Resistance is
like a thin layer of ice across a shallow pool of water. As
soon as you go through, you feel solid ground beneath your

feet. Exercise 7, Solid as a Rock, can help you face up to resistance as well as doubts about your courage, strength, and stability.

You create room for feelings while you set boundaries on behavior.

⊕ *Exercise 7 for Parents: Solid as a Rock*

⊕ *Exercise 3 for Teens: Solid as a Rock*

PART TWO

Compassion

The skies are an enchanting blue.
The water mirrors
little white clouds
illuminated by the sun,
transparent, gold-rimmed
creatures of the sky.
Slowly,
soothing and serene,
they float past,
leaving no trace,
only awareness:
they pass

—*Eline Snel*

Compassion is in all of us. We all possess the natural instinct to ease pain and suffering and to foster happiness. The challenge when raising children is to maintain a balance between your open mind (mindfulness) and your warm heart (heartfulness). This balance should enable you to feel deeply and act wisely, in relation both to yourself and to others, including your children. It is a huge challenge, and you may find it particularly tough when your children reach puberty. But when the going is rough, compassion is all the more important—for your children as well as for yourself.

six

WARMLY EMBRACING A CRISIS

*I*t is about three in the morning. It is chilly. I wake with a jolt, and immediately a terrible feeling comes over me. Is she home? When I tiptoe into her room, I see that her bed has not been slept in. I knew it.

I feel as if all the life has just been sucked out of me; I am exhausted. This is not the first time; it has been going on for months. Why is this happening? Alcohol, the wrong friends, trouble at school . . . not to mention her restlessness. The minute she gets home, she wants to get away again, away from all things safe and familiar, away from everything dear to her. There is no point in locking the doors; she escapes through the window.

I want to stop it, hold her and protect her from male predators and drug dealers. Maintain control. But nothing I do has the slightest effect. I feel like a failure, and it scares me, because I have to help her. I ought to know how to support her, but I do not have the answer.

Henk, my husband, has woken up as well. By the look and sound of it, he feels far from drained. He is furious. He is ranting and raving: "She's out again? Who does she think she is? This is too much. It's destroying me, and I won't let it happen." And then, for the first time, I see him cry. Big, powerless, paternal tears roll down his unshaven cheeks. All the pent-up tension, the sorrow, and the powerlessness are coming out now.

We get dressed without a word and go out into the night to search for our daughter. She is at a house party, and there are no adults on the premises. When she spots us, she tries to run away and shrieks: "I'm not coming with you if that's what you're thinking."

Despite the crisis, I am starting to become aware of something. Something soft, something alive, something powerful is growing inside me. I see her confusion, hear her cries to be let go, but suddenly I also perceive her vulnerability. It hurts me deeply to see her struggling and suffering so much. I feel for her intensely, but I also know that I will not give in. I am responsible for bringing her to safety as long as she is unable to do so herself.

Something has changed. Because I put myself in her position, I no longer feel just my own pain and fear but hers as well. It makes a world of difference. I am no longer against her but with her. And she feels it too.

⊕ *Exercise 8 for Parents: Putting Yourself
in Your Child's Shoes*

SURVIVAL

Children and parents, as well as teachers and social workers, often react instinctively and automatically in a conflict or a crisis. We have not lost our old survival instincts, our tendency to fight, flee, or freeze. We trivialize things, declare war on others, or ignore or belittle something or someone. And well into adulthood we continue to declare war on ourselves, to subject ourselves to callous criticism or, alternatively, to talk ourselves into a sense of superiority: at least I am doing better than . . . This feels familiar to us, since many of us received a lot of unnecessary criticism from our parents: "Wipe that grin off your face," "Straighten up, you slouch," or "With those grades no company will ever hire you." If you constantly hear that your negative qualities outweigh the positive, you will eventually come to believe it. A lack of self-confidence and self-worth can lead children to make the wrong decisions, choose the wrong friends, look for all kinds of ways to numb or obscure the unpleasant feelings, or hurt themselves in some other way. It can even get to the point where children lose the will to live. The number of children with suicidal thoughts is increasing at an alarming rate worldwide.

Things have been going well for a couple of days now. We are connecting more often. It is as if the sun has suddenly appeared through a small gap in the clouds. She is back, the daughter I used to know. Honest, precocious, brave, strong, and warm. We hold each other, saying how much we love each other and how much we miss this kind of contact. She tells me that she cannot help herself. She has no idea what keeps coming over her; it is as if she were taken over by somebody else. And when that happens she feels despondent, she says, empty inside, and she does not want to live anymore. When I ask her if she really wants to die, she shakes her head: "No, not really." But something is hurting her, and she wants to be rid of it. She has no idea what this something is, but it is driving her away instead of back home. And this something is a lot stronger than she is.

And then the trouble flares up again.

CRADLING YOUR HEART

I cradle my heart and keep connecting it with hers, as well as with those of others parents all over the world who are going through something similar. I am one of millions of parents of millions of teenagers with similar behavior. I also connect with them. It helps; it comforts me.

And it is all I can do for now. However difficult and sad it may be, I cannot make it any easier, only more bearable. Self-compassion works a bit like an oxygen mask; in a crisis you are meant to put your own on first before helping your children. We need self-compassion to keep breathing, to avoid getting trapped in fear and shocking images of children running away from home, doing drugs, self-harming, or even taking their own lives.

Self-compassion softens our tendency toward self-criticism, so we can rehabilitate our thoughts and feelings—thoughts like: "I really ought to know. . . ," "After all, I'm her parent and I've been a therapist for thirty years." Or the feelings of shame that arise when everything goes wrong again. When you have compassion for yourself, you have a place where warmth, peace, and emotional stability prevail.

Self-compassion teaches you to live life without a "space suit," sensitive to your own and other people's suffering—with empathy instead of pity, with the ability to imagine yourself in the other's position, without being overwhelmed or carried away by the emotions.

Self-compassion teaches you to look and listen differently, to observe without judgment but with respect for the intricacies of life. And with self-compassion you remain in touch with your inner source of wisdom and your intuition, which—like the North Star—can point you in the right direction and help you find your way. What next?

The moment arrives when Henk and I realize we cannot do this on our own. We need professional help. What follows is a lengthy and often frustrating search that takes us to various agencies with lots of red tape and labels. But in the end we find him, the person who is prepared to really look at our daughter, to really listen to her, and who wants to help her find herself again. Somebody who puts his heart and soul into his job and who will not walk away before our daughter has found her footing again. Before long, there is more laughter when we pick her up from her sessions. We are also advised to do something fun together every week—and our daughter gets to choose what that is.

seven

COMPASSION FOR YOURSELF

We are only people. We have shortcomings as well as virtues. We cannot always succeed, and we will continue to encounter situations that shatter the illusion of perfection and control.

Luckily, we have more to offer ourselves and others than just fighting, fleeing, or freezing. To begin with, we can offer ourselves the safety and solicitous care we need in difficult times. Who else knows best what you are going through behind your mask of "everything is under control"? Who is familiar with your clever escape routes, feels the full force of your pain, and is always available for friendly and sympathetic support, at all hours of the day? You are.

At first it may seem unnatural and strange to be gentle and considerate to yourself, especially when you think you have made a mess of things and you keep feeling the irresistible urge to put yourself down. But you can practice looking at yourself in a different light, just like a mother and father look at their newborn child. As soon as you start to show some understanding for your own hurt feelings, stop fighting your conflicted feelings, and start looking for happiness, you create room for developing friendliness and playfulness, and for nurturing a greater tolerance for your own and other people's shortcomings and feelings—not instantly, but over time. And then one day, before you know it, you will find yourself smiling in situations that you wouldn't have previously.

⊕ Exercise 9 for Parents: Cradling Your Heart

Once we have managed to restore the balance in our hearts and minds, compassion can grow, little by little. If we are used to rejecting ourselves, this is not easy. Our automatic reactions originate in places that are still dark with sorrow or where old injuries remain unhealed. But it is worth the effort: as long as we keep rejecting ourselves and do not admit or acknowledge our own sorrow or pain, we will often, sometimes unknowingly, reject our children's sorrow and pain.

MINOR INCIDENTS

Jim is in his sophomore year of high school. He has just turned sixteen. With his trousers riding dangerously low on his hips, his red-and-black dyed hair in long, trendy bangs hanging over his eyes, and a T-shirt that says REST IN PIECES, *he turns up for an intake interview for the Mindfulness Matters! program. He claims that nothing is really wrong but that his mother, irritating as she is, thinks it is time for a change. Asked why he wants to do the training, he says: "I feel bad, tired, down sometimes. I'm not sleeping well, and I'm having more and more trouble concentrating."*

In response to my question about how things are at home, he says a little flippantly: "Oh, everything's fine at home. Just some minor incidents." When I press him on this, he tells me that he has difficulties with the fact that his mother does not trust him. She checks up on everything, including his homework and his room. And she is always criticizing the people he hangs out with. "It's tough," he mutters. "But I guess that's how it goes."

"What do you usually do when something's tough?" I ask him casually.

He shrugs his skinny shoulders and says with a dark look in his eyes: "Oh, I'll grab the first thing I see and smash it to pieces."

Jim ends up in a mindfulness group with two other young guys and three girls. Their shared symptoms are fear of failure, mood swings, and poor concentration. They all have difficulty managing their intense feelings. They vent their emotions, immediately and impulsively, just like their parents sometimes do.

COMPASSION FOR FEELINGS

During our fourth session, Jim talks about a terrible argument he and his mother had earlier that day. She was furious about his bad grades and kept yelling that he would never get anywhere. That he would have to work as a supermarket cashier for the rest of his life if he didn't change. And what nice girl would ever be interested in him? His anger rising, Jim ran up to his room. "My first thought was: 'I want to break something, I'm going to smash up my desk. That will force her to come upstairs.' Instead something else happened. I was reminded of the ice cube and of feeling your feelings. I approached this horrible feeling and realized I was really sad. I felt alone. It was really awful. I was shaking all over, and I got that familiar sensation in my stomach that I always get when nobody understands me. Every time I feel like that, I smash something, but this time I didn't—I started breathing. It was really weird, but the breathing brought me into something like the eye of the storm, where everything was quiet. I didn't have to do anything except wait for it to pass. It was the first time I didn't break anything. But I felt exhausted afterward."

Jim sighs, as does the rest of the group, which has been listening with rapt attention. I congratulate him on noticing his thoughts in such a difficult situation and on feeling the sadness hidden underneath his anger. The others think it is cool that he managed to do it.

"It was only the first time," he says softly.

We talk some more about feelings of anger and sadness, which are familiar to everyone. We all agree that it helps to go back to your breath, even in the middle of a crisis. Or perhaps especially in the middle of a crisis.

We look at our children through tinted glasses. When the color of the lenses is determined by our own earlier experiences of pain, sorrow, or hurt, it will have a huge influence on our reactions during moments of stress. This will continue until we heal those feelings. This healing process begins with feeling compassion for those parts of yourself that are still suffering. You come up against these places in yourself when your automatic reactions to your child are too harsh, angry, compliant, indifferent, or unsubtle or are prompted by powerlessness.

I speak to Jim's mother on a regular basis. She has done the mindfulness program three times now and frequently attends quiet-contemplation days. "To keep my house in good order," she says with a smile. She makes a little more progress every time and is now able to face up to the loneliness she often felt as a child. She can admit and feel this old pain and comfort herself.

She grew up in a family of six children, including an autistic brother. There was a lot of yelling, criticizing, and tiptoeing around each other's emotions. Her brother always came first. He was often aggressive, while she had to contain herself and suppress her emotions. And she had a lot of emotions.

"Why don't you just finish school and not cause trouble, so we'll have one less thing to worry about," her father used to say. And so she made herself invisible. She never received

compliments, and she developed a strategy whereby, as soon as she felt uncomfortable, she would lash out. It would bring her attention, albeit not the kind she so badly needed. Quite the opposite.

When we look at our own inner world, get to know it, and learn to love it, we also create the space to love our children's inner worlds too. We cannot do this without self-love, because how can we reach out to a child if we keep ourselves at arm's length? How can we treat our child with respect if we are engulfed by shame, guilt, or self-criticism? Compassion for ourselves is the firm foundation for compassion for others. You can practice compassion in all sorts of little, everyday ways. Exercise 10, The Desire to Be Happy, can help.

⊕ *Exercise 10 for Parents: The Desire to Be Happy*

Jim and his mother are getting along a lot better now. Jim no longer feels the need to smash things, while his mother has less reason to vent her anger. Not only have they become more considerate of each other, they also have a greater understanding of each other's emotions.

Compassion for ourselves or others does not mean trying to fix everything. That would be impossible anyway. But instead of either turning away from your child or trying to solve things for her or him, you could offer your warm, open heart.

eight

OFFERING YOUR HEART

F *ourteen-year-old Eva is messaging friends on Facebook during recess when a girlfriend calls her over. She walks straight over to her friend but forgets to lock her tablet. In a split second a boy from her class snatches her tablet off the table and types a couple of lines before putting it back. A few seconds later all the teachers in school, her parents, grandparents, and other relatives receive the message that Eva has had sex with some of the teachers. A picture of Eva in a skimpy bikini is attached, inviting anyone who wants to get it on to phone Eva.*

Feeling distraught and powerless, Eva bikes home. "I'm never going back to that school!" keeps echoing in her head. "Never, ever."

Luckily, her mother is home, and she hears Eva out without immediately passing judgment on the Internet, on social media, on Eva's classmates, or on Eva herself. With an open and compassionate heart, she listens to her daughter and feels the pain and deep shame without attempting to do anything to resolve it or to lessen the pain. This is not the moment for that.

She listens and deliberately resists every impulse to express her opinion. At the same time, she can feel in her own heart and stomach the betrayal that has devastated her daughter. Conscious of this pain, she accompanies her daughter on this first major confrontation with injustice and betrayal. She listens. Unconditionally.

More often than not, parental care requires nothing but a space in which children can be themselves in everything they go through. And all you need to give in this open space is nonjudgmental attention. It is about offering your heart without restrictive ideas, prejudices, criticism, or stereotyping.

TIME-OUT AT HOME
A Tale of Two Wolves

As soon as you notice that within your heart the drawbridges are being raised and the ramparts fortified again, and that you are retreating from your heart, you may want to try to make a different choice.

Consider the following Native American story.

A grandfather is teaching his grandson about life. "A battle is raging inside me," he tells the boy. "Two wolves are locked in a terrible fight. One wolf is a troublemaker. He is often unfriendly; quick to lose his temper; and filled with impatience, envy, anger, and greed. He is also domineering and self-centered. And when others do not accept this, he plays the victim or flies into a rage. He never really listens, always thinks he is right, knows everything better, and feels superior.

"The other wolf is good. He is patient and listens before he speaks. He is honest, open, caring, and sweet. And not only that, he also has a sense of humor and accepts situations for what they are. He is upbeat, likes to see the best in people, and never gossips behind anyone's back. He is dependable and trustworthy."

The grandson listens attentively, thinks about what he has heard, and then asks his grandfather: "So who's going to win the fight?" The old man smiles and responds: "The wolf I feed the most."

If you have the time, you may want to reread the story and think about certain situations in your child's life in which you have been feeding either one or the other wolf. Perhaps your attention immediately turns to situations in which you wish you had acted differently or better. Perhaps it turns to things you feel ashamed of or guilty about. This is how our mind works: the situations in which we think we fell short are the ones we remember best. Therefore I advise you to linger on the countless moments you *were* there for your child. The child's first day in school, your warm arms around heaving shoulders, and your comforting words: "I'll always come back for you. I'll never leave you." Reflect on the many transitions you have been through together, from pregnancy to birth and up to the present day. What a precious time you have together.

Which quality of the good wolf inside you would you like to feed a bit more? Is it humor, patience, cheerfulness, openness, self-acceptance? Something else? Select a quality and a moment when you would like to work on it. During early-morning stress, for example, or during a conflict.

Which bad-wolf qualities could do with less feeding? Knowing everything better? Not listening? Passing negative judgment on yourself or your child? Something else? Again, select a moment when you could decide not to do, say, or express something.

Feeding the positive works wonders, as does mindful attention. Spending a few minutes every day on the qualities of the wolf of your choice is all it takes. What you feed is what grows; what you do not pay attention to withers and dies.

nine

THE ART OF GOOD CONVERSATION

Every human being longs to really be heard. We all want to be seen, understood, and valued. Proper listening is often a lot more important than offering solutions or dishing out well-intentioned advice.

It is not easy to be fully present in a conversation. What you say is not always what is heard. And what you hear is not always what was actually said. Once your children hit puberty, you may well discover just how incredibly difficult communication can be. When our children are little, they are adaptable. More often than not they will do as you say, and during those years you are the center of their world, no question about it. All of this changes during puberty. Children become critical, start seeing things as black or white, develop their own strong opinions, and will not hesitate to unleash those opinions on you and on your performance. Teenagers who think they know better than you can be pretty irritating. However, with their original ideas and views, they can also be absolutely fascinating and incredibly sweet. Also, they really need you as a sounding board, not only to have someone to rebel against, but also to get a sense of the impact and value of their truth.

If you keep harping on about something, they will give it to you straight: "Okay, is that the end of your lecture? Can I go now?" Raising their eyes to heaven, they will conclude that you are a lost cause or just shrug their shoulders and give up. Sometimes they are surprised, for instance, when they realize you are not that bad after all and they can talk to you about sex, drugs, and other sensitive subjects. Your example, and the way you hold them accountable for their own actions, provides them with a kind of internal script. Through reiteration and candid conversations about what is and is not allowed, they learn to listen—to you and to their maturing self.

Whatever they say, shout, or choose to ignore, the teenagers in your household do not have it in for you. They love you. You are the most important person in their life, and they badly need your presence, vision, and compassion. They just do not want anyone in the world to know it.

Communication may seem simple, but it rarely is. Sometimes we unknowingly copy the way we were or weren't listened to when we were young.

Seventeen-year-old Sophie asks: "Mom, have you seen my pocket calendar? It was on the table a second ago." Her mother replies irritably: "You never clean up after yourself. No wonder you're always losing things." Sophie is surprised: "All I wanted to know was . . ."

Even in ideal situations, when you both genuinely want to know what the other means, talking and listening can cause misunderstanding. What you hear is not always what the other is saying; it is often what you *think* the other person is saying. The exercise on page 71 makes this all too clear.

YOU HEAR ME, BUT YOU'RE NOT LISTENING

Caroline comes bounding down the stairs, three steps at a time, and starts gushing about her new boyfriend, who has just texted her a declaration of love. Suddenly she stops talking and shouts at her mother, who is in the same room but doing something else: "Mom, I'm telling you something important!"

"I hear you," her mother says.

"Sure, but you're not listening. You never do when I've got something important to say to you." Her mother frowns and then resumes what she was doing.

Listening begins with the conscious choice to start listening. This is true for all forms of communication. Of course, teenagers themselves struggle to really listen. You can tell them a hundred times a day to shut the door, switch off the light in the hallway, take their sweaty uniform out of their gym bag and put the bag away. They are masters of the art of selective listening. Teenagers are accustomed to rapid digital traffic with log-in names and acronyms but not to present-moment awareness. Yet they still need to be heard.

LISTENING ATTENTIVELY

You could, as you are reading this, put the book down for a moment. You could close your eyes and choose to just listen. What do you hear? What are those sounds around you? Are they loud or soft? Are they far away or close? Are they in front of you or behind you? Or above you perhaps? Perhaps you can hear the sound of a bird, the tapping of the rain, the whispering of the wind. Or maybe you are hearing completely different things.

Some sounds are pleasant to the ear, like some kinds of music or a birdsong; others are less so: a roaring motorcycle and a dentist's drill spring to mind. The noise of a loud TV or a ringing in your ears can be disruptive, while the murmuring of the sea or sounds of silence calm you down. When you practice listening, you will discover just how rapid, changeable, and unavoidable all of your reactions are. Your mind comes up with its own interpretations and meddles in everything. Your mind gets worked up during the day, but also at night. If you do the same, you will wear yourself out.

TWO TIME-OUTS AT HOME
Time-Out at Home 1: The Floor Plan

You will need pen and paper.
Duration: 10–15 minutes per person; then you swap roles.

This game is for the parent(s) and teen(s) to play together. Even though two people live in the same home and know it well, it's interesting to note how each person's perspective can differ. One person is A, the other B. A and B sit back-to-back. A talks while B listens and draws; no questions are allowed.

As soon as everybody is seated and B has pen and paper ready, A begins describing the layout of the ground floor of the house where he or she lives in as much detail as possible (entrance, living room, kitchen, and so on). B draws the floor plan based on A's description. When the time is up, B shows her or his drawing. How accurate is it? What was said and what did you hear? What did you substitute based on what you thought the other person meant?

Time-Out at Home 2: Keeping a Tally

Keep a tally today of how often you pass judgment on what you hear. Put a mark on your hand or a piece of paper when it happens—not because it is unacceptable, but just out of interest, to get to know the nature of your mind. So do it with a smile. Keep your pencil handy and keep a tally: are you present or absent? Judgmental or not?

The purpose of listening attentively is not so much to calm your mind or notice as many sounds as possible as to become aware of your mind's reactions to those sounds.

LIKE A SUGAR CUBE

Everything your child says or does can evoke a range of thoughts and feelings in you. Your ability to listen depends on your awareness of this and on your ability to stay in touch with both yourself and your child without jumping to conclusions. It is perfectly normal to have interpretations ("You seem to think . . ."), judgments ("You never do a thing"), or preconceived notions ("This attitude won't get you anywhere!"). They color the minds of all of us, all the time. But you need not always react to them. Just observe them. Notice the mood swings, the disappointment, the anger, and the frustration taking shape in your mind, and then watch your mind drawing conclusions and finding solutions, after which everything dissolves again like a sugar cube in a cup of hot tea. By regularly listening to your inner sounds, you will become better attuned to the often nonverbal messages from your teenage child and more likely to notice the underlying tone of your own reactions.

LISTENING TO YOUR CHILD

Genuine communication with your children not only is important for now but also creates a firm foundation for the child's later communicative skills. But that is not to say that you should be available twenty-four hours a day like some kind of emergency-response center.

These are the principles for genuine communication with your child:

Take your child seriously
Talk with respect and honesty
Put off giving ready-made answers
Ask yourself whether your words are helpful or
    hurtful
Be prepared to listen to what you may not want to
    hear

We can connect with one another through eye contact, the tone of our voices, written notes, feelings, unconscious motivations, body language, and gestures. But a connection transforms into real contact only when you involve your heart and you talk *with* rather than *at* one another.

Sixteen-year-old John does not talk much—at home or during the sessions in my practice. But then a communication exercise unexpectedly unleashes a torrent of words. It has become painfully clear to John that his father has never really talked with him, even though they have been living under the same roof forever.

"He's just not interested in me, only in himself," John concludes sadly. "He never, and I mean never, asks me how I am doing, who my friends are, whether I've got a girl-

friend, or if I can handle it all, my homework and every-
thing. All he's interested in are my achievements and my
grades. Not me."

And then he falls silent again.

When I ask him gently how he is handling this, he answers:
"I just shut myself off. I don't talk to him."

When I inquire about the effect this has on him, he says
"Oh, you know," shrugs his shoulders, and stares at the floor.
Our contact is minimal, with only a thin, invisible thread con-
necting us. And so we sit together for a while, without a word,
and without any advice from me. This is a precious moment
to me. Then suddenly John gets up, takes my hand, and says:
"Thanks for listening. See you next week."

I thank him for his openness and his story and tell him he
can call me anytime he needs a listening ear. He nods.

TIME-OUT AT HOME
How Was It for You?

What were your experiences of "being heard" during puberty? Were you given the space to speak freely? Or to
remain silent if you did not feel like talking? What memories surface when you think back to communication with
your parents when you were young? Which of these are
fond memories? And what would you like to do differently
yourself?

Children—the grown-ups of the future—shut themselves off when they are not heard or when they think they will not be heard. They need confirmation of what their inner voice tells them. When that confirmation is not forthcoming, they no longer trust that inner voice telling them they are doing something too dangerous or too tough or simply unpleasant. And so they also miss the warning signs when they or others cross boundaries. They may feel it, but they fail to respond to it. How can they take themselves seriously if their parents don't?

The inner voice and intuition of children must be encouraged so they learn to trust it. For this they need a safe space where they can afford to be insecure, misunderstand things, or make mistakes without eliciting negative reactions. Adults can give them that space. And as soon as teenagers are given the space to debate, question your opinions, and express their own truth, as well as being given the opportunity to make choices other than the ones you would make, their self-confidence will grow. And with it the ability to be themselves, thus reducing the feeling that they are supposed to grow up to be someone else, that they have little choice but to grow up according to the values and standards of the adults around them.

⊕ *Exercise 11 for Parents: The Art of Listening*

⊕ *Exercise 4 for Teens: Are You Listening to Me?*

Proper Listening Is an Art

When I ask you to listen to me
and you start giving advice,
you have not done what I asked.

When I ask you to listen to me
and you begin to tell me why
I shouldn't feel that way,
you are trampling on my feelings.

When I ask you to listen to me
and you feel you have to do something to
    solve my problems,
you have failed me,
So please, just listen
and hear me.
And if you want to talk,
wait a few minutes for your turn,
and I promise I'll listen to you.

—*Leo Buscaglia*

I'M LISTENING, EVEN WHEN YOU'RE NOT SAYING ANYTHING

A silent presence in the face of a teenager's reticence to communicate is also an important—but difficult—form of communication.

A mother tells me about her frustration and her trouble accepting that her fifteen-year-old son simply does not talk to her.

"He excludes me," she says. "He's done so for years. He's always rebelling—against school, against teachers, against everything and everyone really—but most of all against us. He accepts no help whatsoever, even though he really needs it. He's angry, contrary, and headstrong. He skips school a lot and does not do his homework. The minute he comes home, he lies down on his bed, no matter how much he has to do. He even tells his friends: "Don't bother talking to them, they're just my parents." He was like this as a small child, but it got worse in his first year at junior high. He's out of control. Social workers have attached all kinds of labels, including ADHD, but that doesn't make communicating any easier. If I so much as smile at him, he flashes me an angry look: 'Don't look at me like that; I can't stand it.'"

When asked if there is anything at all that elicits a positive response, she immediately answers: "Yes, touch. It's the only thing he'll put up with. At night, before he goes to bed, he sometimes asks for a massage. And sometimes I ask him if he wants one. His back and shoulders are always really tense. These are our brief, wonderful moments of true contact." Without words, gentle, loving fingers move across hard, intransigent muscles under tight skin. Again and again. Without words, but with contact and lots of love.

This form of communication requires courage and compassion, including self-compassion. It takes courage to maintain contact irrespective of personal expectations. It is all about being present in the now, without an objective, without the interference of ideas about how things ought to be or how it never was. And you need self-compassion for all of those moments when you get angry or frustrated because you are resisting how things are now.

THE DIGITAL AGE

I often detect a note of nostalgia in parents' voices when they tell me that the contact with their children changed when they hit puberty. It was no longer what it used to be. Teenagers become more taciturn, responding with the standard "nothing" when asked if anything is wrong. They have better contact with their phone than with you. What can you do?

"I'll call you later," Anne says to her friend when they leave school and cycle home in opposite directions.

"Why are you calling her?" I ask my daughter when she picks up her phone the minute she gets home. "You've seen and spoken to her all day, right?"

"Talking on the phone is different," she kindly explains. "You wouldn't understand. Sorry." She raises her hand, palm forward, in an elegant, apologetic gesture, as if to say: "Talk to the hand, the face ain't listening." She bounds up the stairs to

her room, where she spends the next hour on the phone. My teenage daughter's first few phone bills came to about half my monthly salary. It took us awhile to realize that we had to clamp down on it.

Armed with Internet and cell phone, teenagers can be in touch 24/7. They can keep each other posted at all times: where they are, who they are with, what they are doing, and how they are feeling. It is also a way of gauging who has influence and how they ought to behave to fit in.

"If I'm not in touch for a couple of days, they think I'm dead," says a friend of our younger son, who has just acquired his first smartphone and is already familiar with the functions that took me years to master.

I nod my understanding. With my dull, standard text messages and only the strictly necessary work-related digital traffic, I am clearly a relic from a different era. But I realize I need to explore the Internet's many attractions, and their dangers, if I want to know what's happening digitally. To my dismay, I stumble across the most horrible things about cyberbullying during my search. I also discover the temptations and the intimate harassment children are exposed to via e-mail. The dangers of child "grooming" have long been underestimated.

I also hear teenagers talk about the horror films they

watch on their cell phones or iPad until the early hours of the morning . . . and then chat about with others. Yet they fail to establish the link between that and the insomnia they experience. A huge number of teenagers have a TV and a computer or a smartphone with Internet in their bedroom. This makes it hard for parents to exercise any control over what programs their teenage children are watching or what time they go to sleep. Let alone with whom they chat.

Finding a way to communicate about this is a huge challenge. Parents' influence wanes as puberty progresses, but old-fashioned face time remains important, talking about everything that is happening on the Internet or about how hard it is for young computer users to assess the veracity of digital information. You also need to get across to your children that while you understand that they do not want you to interfere in their world, you have no choice in some cases.

MASTERS OF COMMUNICATION

Teenagers are masters of communication. They make a conscious decision to speak or remain silent, which requires that the parents be flexible and agile in their responses to their child. They are online all day long, are highly skilled at developing quick and effective "digispeak," and keep up to date with everything that happens in the digital world. They get a lot out of it. But it is also getting harder for them to break free from the compulsion of always being online. Many do not even go to sleep without their phone ("It's got an alarm clock, you know"). And they struggle to have a normal conversation, that is, to be present "in the flesh" for more than a couple of minutes.

Communicating with teenagers requires a lot of attention. But it is also very rewarding. There is the lopsided, insecure grin with the clear message: "Promise me you'll wait at the corner over there when you pick me up me, okay? I really don't want them to see you!" Then there are the intimate moments when, head over heels in love, they sit down on the edge of your bed and ask expectantly: "What do you think of her?"

There will inevitably be moments when communication grinds to a halt, a conversation ends in a war of words, or disagreements about media use go on for days. At such moments you may find it helpful to experiment with in-action. It will do you and your child a world of good to stay where you are. Here, in this moment, with this feeling, with this tendency to slip into a familiar communication pattern, to force something, or to give in too soon. Notice your habit of renegotiating or imposing rules instead of discussing them with each other. If you can wait until the turbulence has subsided, the right answer will present itself. Patience, trust, and letting go of the idea that we can control everything are extremely rewarding.

The right answer will come as long as you are prepared to wait. Mindfulness gives you the courage to wait out the storm at sea or to keep your ship in the harbor and not set sail again until the worst is over.

TIME-OUT AT HOME
Communicating

There are a few things that are helpful to keep in mind as you strive to keep communication with your teenager open and productive.

First, the value of a good, long conversation with their parents and peers alike is something that your teenage children will likely not recognize until well after high school. During puberty, it's only their opinion that matters. Communication between teenagers and adults requires detachment, mutual respect, and a degree of casualness. You will often get more out of a brief exchange while walking the dog, during a drive or a snatched moment on the doorstep, or while having a conversation with someone else, than from the words: "We need to talk."

Also, no matter how different the interests of you and your teenage children are, it is vital that you keep showing a genuine interest. When you ask thoughtful questions—rather than cross-examine—teenagers are sometimes willing to abandon their fight against communicating with you. It can be difficult to hit the right notes, to maintain the appropriate distance, and to avoid the pitfall of feeling attacked by the other person's disrespectful tone.

If there is tension about an issue that cannot be resolved very easily (computer use, boundaries, household tasks, nights out, alcohol, and so on), start by looking at your intention, your initial impulse to say something, and your nonverbal attitude. What can you notice about the sound and tone of your voice? What questions are you asking your teenager to find out what's really going on? Become aware of all of those moments when you expect yourself to help, want to resolve something right away, or want to impose your own will where you may not need to. Also note what is happening to your child. Is there resistance? Is the distance between you increasing or decreasing? How do you react to discussions or verbal abuse? See if you can put off giving a solution to a problem despite the anxiety produced by the lack of a ready-made response or a plan.

You usually try really hard to do or say the right thing. Try to avoid doing that every once in a while. If you practice this, the right answer may come automatically and at the right time if you are prepared to wait for it. And so a different kind of communication will emerge: a less impulsive one, inspired by connectedness rather than old familiar patterns.

PART THREE

Trust

If only we had the patience of a caterpillar in a cocoon, waiting to transform into a butterfly. If only we
had the trust of a newborn child. Or if only we could
let go with the wisdom of a leaf in the fall. Our lives
would surely be easier.

The sentences above are something I wrote in *Sitting Still
Like a Frog*. When your child is in puberty, the trust you
once took for granted is likely to take a beating; the patience of a caterpillar is sometimes sorely lacking; and you
would rather hold on than let go and take a backseat. Hor-
monal changes in your child can cause huge mood swings
and impulsive or irresponsible behavior. You would like to
know more about the new friends your child hangs out
with night after night, but you are rarely told anything. The
neural network that assesses risk is only partially developed
in the teenage brain. Optimum vigilance and supervision
will get you far as a parent—and trust, in your child and
yourself, will get you a little further still.

ten

TRUST IN YOUR CHILD,
TRUST IN YOURSELF

When your child is a teenager, as a parent you will be asked to let go of your reins of control in ways you never expected or anticipated. You will need to trust your child as they deal with social and school-related situations, take chances, make mistakes—and then fix them, explore, and find out who they are as individuals separate from you. And you will need to react with compassion and solidity even when situations go awry. You will also need to trust in yourself as a parent in just the same ways—as you struggle, fail, set limits, and feel adrift at times. Approaching both your child and yourself with compassion in these myriad situations is the key.

Niles, who is a father to two fantastic teenage sons, lacked the trust of his own parents when he was young. "I wouldn't do that if I were you; it's not your thing," was their invariable response to practically all of his ideas and plans. Although his experience made him extremely insecure, it has now become

*the basis for giving his sons all the trust they need. Not blind
trust, but trust in his children's good nature.*

*Sara, a high school sophomore, wants to spend the night
with her new boyfriend, who is a senior. Her mother is ada-
mant that she cannot go. "Invite him over to our house," she
suggests. "He's more than welcome here, but I don't want you
to spend the night there."*

*Sara snaps at her mother: "You don't trust me, do you? You
never do! It's not as if I'm doing anything wrong. He loves me
and I love him, and this is what we agreed. I'm not going to
phone and cancel now. I'd look like an idiot!"*

*Sara's mother does not rise to the bait and looks her daugh-
ter openly and respectfully in the eye. Calmly she says that she
does trust Sara and does not doubt her good intentions at all
but that she does not trust the situation. If she stays the night,
Sara might end up feeling compelled to do things she is not
ready for or might regret afterward.*

*Sara flies into a rage, but her mother stands her ground.
Sara is not allowed to go.*

The process of building trust is a gradual and extremely
delicate one. It begins in childhood, when you are fed when
you are hungry, comforted when you are sad, and given
unconditional support when you need it. And when you
know you are loved, whether or not you make mistakes
or fail to meet high expectations, the world is yours and

you can spread your wings. But building trust is not always quite so easy, nor can it be taken for granted.

Sooner or later the first cracks will appear in what was once so good or perfect. And it may not stop at cracks; sometimes there will be huge ruptures, entire fault lines across the once firm foundation of domestic happiness. But what exactly is cracking? Which foundation is shaking? Could there be a treasure buried underneath?

THE WARM ACCEPTANCE OF IMPERFECTION

The rain is pouring down, but it is nothing compared with the weather inside me. I have been anticipating this moment of despair for days. And now it has come. It feels like fear, like panic, like falling through space, not knowing where I will end up. But at the same time it feels familiar, like an old friend I have not seen in a long time, one I have deliberately held at arm's length. "This is vulnerability," I mutter to myself. Vulnerability, I open myself up to you, connect with you, admit you into every one of my cells.

And then I notice my husband coming in. He wraps a warm arm around me and sees me in all of my emotional nakedness. Unspoken comfort enters my being, in this moment when I am feeling vulnerable.

At this moment, when my expectations about "good" motherhood have hit rock bottom, I come face-to-face with my imperfections. I feel like a failure. Feelings of shame and guilt fight for primary position, because I can no longer guarantee my daughter's safety. What a disaster! And many of the people close to Henk and me do not mince words. They all know better than we do and so reinforce my doubts. Some of their judgments are harsh. Shouldn't I have seen this coming a long time ago? Perhaps I should have been tougher. Perhaps if I hadn't done this, then . . .

I let my tears run freely as I roam the supermarket aisles in search of groceries. There is chaos in my head. The comfortable, coherent person I thought I was is riddled with cracks. But then suddenly a line surfaces from the blurry confusion in my head: "In order to love, you need to be at home in yourself."

The rain outside stops. Nothing has been resolved yet; in fact, nothing has changed. But I surrender. I stop fighting. I give up trying to be perfect, wanting to do things better. Somewhere deep inside, I feel a sense of release bubbling up.

In this situation, surrendering is not the same as giving up. Nor is it the same as loss or resignation. What is abandoned is the fallacy, the random image of how we ought to be or how we ought to respond. The other things that are jettisoned are alienation between me and my daughter and, in fact, everything that keeps people apart: expectations, differences of opinion, and entrenched ideas about what is good and what is bad.

We look at each other, see each other, embrace, and then . . . then she leaves us. She is only fourteen but she is determined to find her way back to herself by moving temporarily into a mental healthcare hospital for treatment. Professional care workers can provide the necessary time, space, and attention. She needs to be away from us for a while. But not without us. We have some extraordinary conversations, and slowly but surely we drop our familiar masks: her tough "I can do it alone; mind your own business" attitude, her indifferent "leave me alone" face, and my "I've got to help you" mask. The conversations are not always pleasant; they are often exhausting and upsetting at the same time, but they are certainly necessary.

The remnants of our mutual value judgments lie in a heap by the wayside, with the filter of "always in control" sitting on top of it. What emerges in its place is breath, space, vulnerability, and strength. Light is beginning to stream through the cracks in our masks. Neither we nor the world has suddenly changed, but our perspective of each other has, and that makes a huge difference. We hear each other and sense each other's proximity and dependence.

We are in contact without holding back. Ideas about what we could or should do next come and go. We practice patience, learn to trust again, and let go of what we should have stopped clinging to a long time ago.

For glimpses into our own labyrinthine depths, it is not always necessary for our whole world to collapse first. We can seize on the minor cracks in our masks as an invitation to truly see and feel ourselves and others and to accept that we need not become perfect—we already are. Vulnerability and imperfection are at the root of self-confidence, connectedness, courage, and compassion. They are the source of wisdom and the beginning of acceptance: the warm acceptance of imperfection.

eleven

DESIRE

We all want the very best for our children's future
Even though we know that the tides are always
changing and that not everything will go as we plan, our
wishes, hopes, and desires for our children are important.
They motivate us to take steps to create a better, safer, and
healthier world. But these desires can also be difficult for
us to navigate—as they can keep drawing attention to what
we do not have rather than to what we do have. How do
you handle them without becoming trapped by what you
badly want but that is still out of reach?

In many cases, our desires can be realized through tar-
geted action. You want to find a good school for your children? Then you can attend open houses, talk to your children about what they want, and then explore together what
might be the best place for them. But there are plenty of
wishes we cannot realize, simply because we lack the power.

The reading on mindfulness and well-being for teachers, deliv-
ered to sixty school principals, has just come to an end when a
woman approaches me. She has tears in her eyes.

"Thank you for the reading." She tells me it has given her confidence.

When I ask her what it was exactly that has given her confidence, she replies: "Just seeing you standing there with your daughter. The two of you together. I haven't had any real contact with my daughter for far too long now. We live in different countries, and I don't really know how she's doing. But now I know there's another way. Looking at the two of you inspires me not to give up but to keep wishing for different times, although I don't know how to achieve it yet." She shakes our hands warmly and heads home with a spring in her step.

ACCEPTANCE, PATIENCE, TRUST, AND LETTING GO

There are so many things we have no influence over: a child contracting a serious illness, parents losing their jobs and not having enough money for a good education, the death of a beloved friend or relative. Or war, the never-ending spiral of violence that causes so much suffering. You would love to change the situation, but you have no control over it.

There is no point in clinging to desires, in continuing to strive for change against your better judgment. If you become trapped by your desires, you can end up frustrated, irritated, apathetic, and angry, which will only make things worse. So what can you do with those intense desires for change, for a better outlook or a more profound insight?

This is where acceptance, patience, trust, and letting

go come into the picture. Acceptance is the inner preparedness to accept that there are some situations in life that are unpleasant, downright painful, or extremely sad. There is nothing we can do about it. Where our children are concerned, acceptance is about recognizing that there are differences between them and us without wanting to change anything or exclude or reject any part of them. We have to accept all of those moments when they refuse to cooperate, be friendly, or do something for us without getting anything in return. But acceptance is also something you need to do with yourself, during all of those moments when you are not quite the perfect parent, during the situations when you run out of patience and you want your expectations to be met.

Patience has to do with our sense of timing and the recognition that everything takes time to be born, grow, heal, or emerge. You cannot really force this. Patience is not about clock time but about the right moment. Giving your child the occasional push in the right direction can help, but so does the patience of the caterpillar that knows it will transform into a butterfly. They always pull it off, those caterpillars, without any noticeable effort. As long as they are given the time to let nature take its course, everything will be all right. Our teenagers, too, need time to grow.

Trust is the experience of a basic feeling of security and the expectation that everything will be all right, even if current circumstances seem to suggest otherwise. Trust enables us to accept the things we cannot control, resign ourselves to the fact that our teenage child needs time, and then wait for the tide to turn. It always does, as long as you are patient. A caterpillar always transforms into a butterfly—you can rely on it—provided the cocoon does not rupture prematurely.

Letting go is the ability not to give in to the need to manipulate or accelerate a process. If we surrender control, we will realize that change does not always take place because we want something to be other than what it is now but because we *know* it will take place. It gives you the freedom to take your own approach to the inevitable ripples in life. At this point it may be worth recalling how much has changed in your own life. Some of it may have gone unnoticed. The following meditation might help you become more conscious of those changes. Maybe someone can read the following meditation to you while you practice it, or, alternatively, you can read the text yourself while taking the occasional break to connect with the memory of a strong desire that you once had.

TIME-OUT AT HOME
Experiencing the Changes in Your Life

Sit down comfortably on a chair or a couch and close your eyes. Direct your attention to the familiar movement of your breath in your belly or your chest. Where do you feel the breath? And how does it feel? Observe the movement of your breath as it is right now, without having to change it. Breathe in and breathe out again. You have all the time in the world to observe these inhalations and exhalations for a while. Be present with them and notice that you are breathing.

Then, when you are ready, you can delve into your memories and pick a moment when you felt a strong desire for change. You need not really hunt for the situation—it will surface. What is coming up? It can be an old memory, a memory from a couple of years back, or a much more recent one. You may remember it as if it were yesterday. Now zoom in on this memory. What was the situation you wanted to see changed? What feelings come to the fore now that you are thinking about it? And what thoughts? Perhaps you are noticing other things. Look at all of the images and memories without letting yourself get carried away by them. Just look at them from a distance. Then slowly pull away from the situation and bring yourself back to the now by focusing on your breathing again. While experiencing the present moment, you can reflect on how things are in your life right now. What has changed between then and now? What has changed in relation to the desire? What role did you play in this? And what role did life play? What else do you notice in connection with your desire and the changes that have taken place in the intervening period?

Deirdre is a young mother of two. After doing this meditation, she tells me with tears in her eyes that, ten years ago, she was in the grip of an intense desire to be cured of breast cancer. Her deepest desire was to see her children grow up. And it happened. Ten years down the line, she is alive and living life to the full. What a change compared with ten years ago. Gratefully, she reflects on her strong sense of vitality and the confidence that is increasing with age. It is a remarkable thing to reflect on.

⊕ Exercise 12 for Parents: Patience, Trust, and Letting Go: The Wishing Tree

⊕ Exercise 13 for Parents and Teenagers: Sleep Tight

The Wishing Tree meditation on the audio download (Patience, Trust, and Letting Go: The Wishing Tree) can help you deal with strong desires that cannot be fulfilled through sheer willpower or a proactive approach. The ancient wishing-tree meditation nourishes the heart, ends the feeling of powerlessness, and offers a comforting and profound insight into the changeability that lies at the root of existence.

Everything changes. By visualizing deep desires and putting them into words, by acknowledging the longing and then letting go again, something changes in and of itself. This is the experience of parents in the training program.

Most of the teenagers in our teen program have never spoken to anyone about their desires. Not even now in their mindfulness group. But when the bell marks the end of their meditation, their faces look mellow, relaxed, and full of confidence.

"That was nice," they sigh. "Can we do this more often?"

Mindfulness exercises will give them the short-term confidence that they can do something about their desires and the long-term confidence that everything will be all right, even if there is nothing they can do.

At the request of many parents and young people, the exercise Sleep Tight has also been included on the download. Sleeping tight has everything to do with cultivating this type of confidence. It is a desire that can be realized—sometimes sooner than you think—with a bit of practice at doing nothing and learning how to stop listening to your thoughts.

When we give ourselves over to life and pass this attitude on to our children, they will learn that it is okay to make mistakes and that it's normal to suffer rejection. You take wrong turns, only to retrace your steps and try another road. There will always be a second chance. You never know what is around the corner. Patience and trust are but a breath away from stress, fear, insecurity, rejection, or the winds of fate, but they give you two strong wings with which to fly.

WHEN DESIRES CLASH

When children are in puberty, the desires of parents may be at odds with those of their children. By accepting this as a normal and common occurrence, you will avoid endless discussions. Things become complicated only when you as a parent expect your child to become someone other than the person he or she is, when you do not trust your child to figure out who he or she is, and when you want your child to become the person you had wanted to be.

In all of these cases, parents start pushing, forcing their child into the heartless world of "not and never will be good enough." "Harder, better, faster," a father yells at his son from the sidelines. So he thinks he knows what his son's dreams are? Did he fail to realize his own?

An interview with a mentor at a leading basketball academy, published in a national newspaper, makes it painfully clear that many parents suffer from "push-and-pull" syndrome. The father of one pupil is determined that one day his son will shine at the Olympic Games. He never had the chance, so now his son will have to make it happen. But the boy has very different ambitions. He likes sports because he enjoys exercise and the element of play, but he is also very good at drawing. In fact, he probably likes drawing better. But the father will not give an inch, forcing the child to go against his nature. He pushes him and pulls him into the all-or-nothing mind-set of future winners and yells at him from the sidelines: "Go on. Don't let them walk all over you. You can do much better than that."

The verbal onslaught continues at home. "You have to really go for it. Top-level sport, isn't for wimps. You won't make it if you carry on like this. You'll be a loser! Is that what you want?"

The child is feeling worse and worse, and his performance is starting to slip. His father fails to notice. And then the child becomes ill with exhaustion. The pressure is too much and the trust sorely lacking. And this does not happen just in the world of sports.

Trust fills us with a sense of hope and feeds the expectation that everything will be all right, even when the current situation seems to suggest otherwise. If you build your confidence in your child, it will develop your child's own self-confidence. We want our children to succeed. And we expect our children to know from an early age what they want to be when they grow up, long before they even know who they are. Both school and society want them to choose a direction and route early on. And because high grades and exam scores matter, your children learn that they stand out from the crowd, they count, by excelling. They measure themselves against others on the basis of their capacity for memorizing information. Mental intelligence gets you far in the world. But what about the other intelligence? The intelligence that is already complete and within you?

The pressure to perform in our culture is unbelievably high—and it's contagious. Everybody gets sucked into it, until you decide to stop having such high expectations and take the time to recognize your child's other intelligences. Such a pause may prompt you to trust that inside each and every child is a work of art waiting to be discovered.

A WORK OF ART IN THE MAKING

A wealthy woman was talking to the great artist Michelangelo. She asked him: "Master, how do you manage to make such amazing works?" Michelangelo replied: "Madam, there is nothing in the mind of man that is not already in the block of stone. It is my job to release what is in the stone with patience, love, and craftsmanship. To see what wants to appear."

What would it be like if we could approach ourselves and our children knowing that deep down inside we all possess a beautiful wholeness that can emerge with patience, love, and personal craftsmanship? Within each of us are hidden talents that can be brought to the surface in thousands of different ways. If, with great patience and love of the material, we keep chiseling away at the exterior of rough stone, determined to extract what is inside, our unadulterated beauty will emerge—luminous, clear, and full of unexpected brilliance. Ready to be polished.

What works of art in the making are hidden beneath the surface of your children? What lies beneath the cool exterior, the tough behavior, or the quiet, obedient feet that are in step with the rest? What is the enduring image even when they do not know what to do with their lives? Or when it turns out they have been lying about where they were? What do you continue to see even when your child's stomach is pumped after too much alcohol? What remains visible underneath the drug use, the tattoos, the apparent docility, the arguments, or the disappointment? What remains alive and well and fundamentally unchanged inside each and every child?

Unlocking someone's full potential is at the heart of all processes of upbringing and raising awareness. It is the essence of development. Sooner or later, every bird has to learn how to fly; it is in the bird's nature. Through trial and error and repeated attempts, it will eventually manage. But that is no guarantee that all flights will be perfect.

twelve

YOUR CHILD'S PATH

In life we rarely get straight to our destination. So much can go right or wrong along the way. Sometimes we have things under control, but often we do not. The road can be surprisingly tortuous, with well-hidden obstacles providing additional challenges. We can learn a lot from this. Solid and well-considered plans may be overshadowed by everything life has in store for us. When we teach our children to take good care of themselves and not to retreat behind high walls of resistance or fear with their sensitive heart, they can catch a glimpse of life's abundance. Life can be lived to the fullest; it is always available and within reach. Whatever our role may be, whatever college degree our children will pursue or not, whatever their health allows or not—there are thousands of different ways to unlock all of their potential. But it is up to the children themselves to spread their wings.

At seventeen, after plenty of detours and perseverance, our daughter, Anne, has managed to finish school. Proudly, she shows off her diploma, which even boasts a couple of As. Back home after the graduation ceremony, she flops down onto the

couch and flashes me a warning look from under her long eye-
lashes. Unlike her brothers, she has no intention of continuing
her studies, but that does not stop me from making an ump-
teenth attempt to persuade her to go to college.

"Oh, no, not again!" she says: "No, I don't want to. I want
to learn from life and not from some professor who thinks he
knows what I want to learn."

When my husband and I, obstinate as we can be, start
talking yet again about what we think is useful, important,
and even necessary if our daughter wants to have even the
remotest chance of getting a good and enjoyable job, she rolls
her big green eyes in desperation. "When will you guys stop
deciding for me what to do with my life? I don't do that to
you, do I?"

It finally sinks in. She is right! What did we see growing
from a very early age? It was this: the remarkable combina-
tion of great independence, incisive self-reflection, dynamism,
and a sense of responsibility, mixed with a great capacity for
love and empathy. We let go of our wish for her to go to a good
college we like the look of—we let it go. But we hold on to the
idea that she will give meaning to her life.

Most children possess their own wisdom. Headstrong
and uninhibited, they show you from a young age what
they know and what treasure they carry within, a treasure
that begs to be discovered. They are all out there, the small,
almost invisible talents as well as the big, obvious ones.

LETTING GO

Puberty is an exciting and intense time for parents and kids. Parents struggle to let go of their view of their child as helpless, unable to make it on her or his own in a world full of imagined abysses and unexpected potential. Comments like "As if you know what's what!" or "You finish your degree first and then we'll talk" only serve to reinforce that view within us—and in our child. If we keep ourselves in check, we can teach our children to trust their feelings. And by that I do not mean they should indulge their emotions, but, rather, they should learn to feel what is going on deep down in their heart and to trust it. This is a precious quality, even when still in its early stages.

Teenagers, especially, need your patience and your trust. All young birds fly the nest before they are ready. They continue their lessons from the ground. Flapping and waddling, surrounded by their parents and by countless dangers, they learn to rely on their own wings. And so it works for teenagers. Their formal upbringing may be over, but the search for their true self continues. Our beautiful task as parents is to be present in this process and to practice acceptance and patience, to have faith and, above all, to let go: to abandon attempts to try to solve everything. Have faith in what's in store. Be receptive, attentive, and curious about everything that is ahead.

THE WINGS TO FLY

The suitcase is packed and sitting in the hallway. Flip-flops, some underwear, a toothbrush, one pair of jeans, a couple of T-shirts, and a sweater. "Travel light" is what she was told, but this seems microlight to me. My maternal concern latches on to the suitcase. "Don't you think you'll need some more . . . ," I try cautiously. But before I can finish my sentence, she wags her finger in front of my face.

"Stop it, will you, Mom? I'm not a child anymore. I've got my own wings to fly." Determined, she slings her backpack onto her back. In it, I know, is a small album with photos of us all and a travel charm that I carefully selected for her. Just in case.

At the airport, the entire family forms a circle around her, with her friends forming a second circle around the first. Good-bye. We touch each other. Our fragile hearts open up, both inwardly and outwardly. One last glimpse and she is off. Barely seventeen and on her way to South Africa. Her deep desire to work with children with HIV/AIDS gives her trip an as yet unknown meaning and direction. She is ready to live life to the full, whatever it may hold.

"Cape Town is great," she texts us twenty-four hours later. In response to my anxious question about why it took so long, she writes casually that she missed her connecting flight. "I was chatting with someone." From then on, the adventures

take place at an almost dizzying speed. She lives on the edge, exploring boundaries and taking risks. But she also discovers her living love for children around the world who are less well off than she.

From Africa she continues her journey. She has developed a taste for it now. Her plans change, aiming restlessly for imaginary dots far beyond the horizon. Over there, far from here, is where she will find happiness. It is warmer and more beautiful over there, the people are nicer, and the chances of happiness greater. Still oblivious to her tendency to find happiness outside herself, she carries on traveling . . . further and further away from herself.

Her search for paradise lasts five years. Following two years in New York, she travels to Ambergris Caye. In her own little restaurant on this small island off the coast of Belize, along one of the world's most beautiful coral reefs, she works incredibly hard. "Not a lot of time to enjoy it," she says when we come to visit her.

Her employees worship her. So do the children on the island. She spends her tip money on books for the kids whose parents cannot afford them. She strikes up close and loving friendships with people of all ages from all four corners of the world.

But the beautiful coast is also home to corruption, to people with too much money drinking themselves into a stupor, and to a flourishing drug trade. During one of the most incredible sailing trips across the azure blue waters of the Caribbean, the truth suddenly hits home: paradise is not a place; it consists of moments. It is the discovery of her life.

THE WAY BACK

She returns home feeling ill and exhausted. She sleeps, eats, and talks. Her remarkable stories are suffused with salty tears of fatigue. Twinges of nostalgia for faraway friends very nearly drive her away again. But not now, later. So what about now? She has sold her restaurant, at a profit, but she has no plan. There is nothing for her mind to look forward to or to escape to. This is a new sensation. And out of this new nothingness emerges a way back. Step by step. To bridge the gap between now and later, she wants to do a mindfulness course with me. She has long been familiar with meditation. It is something we have done for years, and sometimes we do it together.

The exercise Sitting Still Like a Frog still helps her calm her busy mind. She registers in a program at my Academy for Mindful Teaching (AMT). She sits. And she breathes. She is aware of her breath in and out. At twenty-two, she is the youngest in the group. Although closer to home and closer to herself, she is traveling once more—inside this time. It is no easy road.

Almost without realizing it, she sets off in a direction with far-reaching consequences for the next couple of years. Bravely, she dives into the deep sea of thoughts and feelings. She discovers her tendency—our tendency—to react immediately, to want to deal with something right away and not accept something someone else says. She notices the workings of her mind when she is about to respond angrily to a text message or give a friend a piece of her mind. She learns to wait until the turbulence has died down and the waters of her mind are clear enough to respond from a mindful position and not out of an impulse that usually creates even more turbulence.

She has a knack for it, I notice. And her self-confidence grows. But it does not happen by itself. Like any muscle, the attention muscle must be trained. During a silent-meditation day something changes. Suddenly she senses what her road will be. At the age of twenty-five I made an inner vow to follow my one true path. And she does the same at the age of twenty-two. She feels a deep inner need to unlock her full potential and tackle the problems she encounters in herself and others with loving, mindful attention. It is a conscious choice. She wants to help as many children as possible understand what is really going on inside them. She wants to hand them the tools they need to connect with the inner genius waiting to be discovered, the rough diamond waiting to be polished, so they can become the person they have been all along.

She cannot let go of the idea. Suddenly she has found a purpose. Like me, she learns most from the many moments when she is not mindful. Surprised by this inattentiveness and amazed by what she sees, hears, feels, and experiences when she is mindful, she continues on her path.

She follows the Mindfulness Matters! child-training program and becomes a certified Mindfulness Based Stress Re-

duction (MBSR) trainer. She starts working as a child coach and becomes the youngest-ever teacher at the AMT. Day after day, she pours her heart and soul into training children across all age categories, at elementary and high schools, at top sports academies, and in special education, as well as in her own practice. She and I work with other terrific colleagues who, under the auspices of the AMT, do great work providing training in the Netherlands and elsewhere.

We see such a transformation—in teenagers and their parents, as well as in ourselves—at the moment we dare to be fully present. It is a labor of love, based on genuine kindness and the capacity for undivided attention to everything that occurs. Doing this, for ourselves and for those we work with, is a privilege.

thirteen

TRUST THROUGH KINDNESS

*M*ark *is a friendly forty-five-year-old man. As a teenager he was badly bullied, and he still feels anxious
whenever he sees a group of people gathered together on the
street. He will head in a different direction, his heart in his
throat: They're not going to chase me, are they? Call me a
wimp again, or worse? At parties he does not mingle with
others for fear of saying something wrong and becoming a
target of ridicule.*

Kindness is one of our most powerful qualities. It is like
a gentle rain that falls everywhere, without missing a single spot. The rain just falls without distinguishing between
here and there. Kindness is inclusive and nonjudgmental
and touches the core of your heart. It enables you to grow
and to learn to trust yourself and others.

Being kind is in everybody's nature. But if that is the
case, why is there still so much hatred, strife, and unfriend-
liness in the world? Virtually all aggression is a reaction to
the feeling or idea of being threatened. Millions of years
ago, our ancestors were exposed to danger. Disease, climate
change, and the battle for scarce food created an "us against

them" mind-set. When life is hard, cooperation within our own group and a hard line against other groups help us to keep going, to survive. With our brains still hardwired with this ancient knowledge, we tend to place people who are not as we would like or expect them to be outside the circle. Us against them.

But for millions of years we have also been blessed with the opposite emotions: kindness, compassion, gratitude, and empathy. While we cannot stop the evil in the world, we can stimulate the good. How do you do this? As with so many other things, it starts with yourself. Practice kindness and notice what happens inside when you are unkind.

PRACTICING KINDNESS

"Constant kindness can accomplish much," Albert Schweitzer once said. Just as the sun melts the ice, friendliness makes misunderstandings, distrust, and hostility evaporate. Kindness toward oneself seems like a perfectly normal and commonsense action, and yet most people struggle with the idea, thinking it strange and inappropriate, a sign of arrogance or self-indulgence. All the children and nearly all the parents I've asked respond to the idea in the same way. Kindness to yourself? "Don't be ridiculous." It takes courage to practice kindness and to give compassionate attention to all of those moments we hurt or inadvertently ridicule each other or do not take each other seriously.

In one of our workshops we handed out wristbands to

the people in each group with the inscription "It's cool to be kind." It was to help everybody with their task, which was to notice when they were unkind and to note the effect this had on them and the other person.

From time to time we are all unkind. It just happens. Sometimes you are ashamed of it, sometimes you do it to recruit allies and exclude others. Sometimes it seems powerful to hurt, belittle, or verbally dominate others. But what happens when others do it to you? How does it feel? How long do the effects last? And what happens to others when you are unkind to them?

You can explore this by using a wristband. Whenever you notice that you are unkind, you turn the wristband inside out, so the text faces inward. The next time you are unkind, you turn it back out again. This exercise is not about telling you that you cannot be unkind—we all are from time to time—but about being aware of it. This awareness can bring about a change—and a big one at that.

A new world opens up when you observe yourself non-judgmentally every day for two weeks and discover that you occasionally say unkind, harsh words for no apparent reason. Many people notice they are particularly unkind to themselves, criticizing themselves nonstop, telling themselves off, or thinking they are stupid or not good enough. Others notice that once they start paying attention, they are less habitually unkind, even to themselves.

It becomes completely quiet when the twenty talented young athletes are instructed to write down a heartfelt compliment for everybody in the classroom. Ouch! This is not as easy as it sounds. They are used to competition, both at home and here. But their focus is usually on achievements, not on compliments.

Gnawing on their pencils, they ponder their task. This is not about cool sneakers or great hair, and it's not about the greatest achievements of the past year either. This is about what you really appreciate, like, or admire about the other person, something you noticed but never mentioned. Afterward, the teacher, who is also taking part, collects the compliments and hands every student the compliments he or she received. They are all surprised, touched, and even a little taken aback by so many beautiful, sincere words—the teacher included.

Kindness, friendliness, is not something that you will run out of—it is a renewable resource that will always be refreshed by kind interactions with others. This is something that you can practice with your teen—especially during challenging times. However, kindness is not the same as praising your children to the highest heavens every time they do or achieve something. Praising does not make them better people, only more insecure ones. It makes them doubt whether they can be just as great and smart again the next time.

Adults who have a history of being bullied or abused

in their past may struggle with the idea of giving themselves or their children the kindness that they need. Some
adults think that retaliating, doing their own bullying and
name-calling, is the answer. I personally disagree. In the
end, violence, verbal abuse, and revenge only lead to more
aggression and resistance, thus keeping the cycle going. The
parable below shows how a snake found a way to open up
to kindness and respect—but to also set limits and keep
himself safe.

THE WISE MAN AND THE SNAKE

*Once upon a time, somewhere on this earth, there was a snake
who was fed up with people screaming and running away
from him. He went into the forest and asked a wise old man
who lived there what he could do to make people fear him
less. The sage gave it some thought and said: "You could try
not to hiss or show your venomous fangs and pretend to be
completely harmless."*

*The snake decided to give it a try, but the strategy backfired.
As soon as the villagers realized that they were no longer in
danger, they started pelting the poor creature with large rocks.
The snake narrowly escaped with his life and writhed back to
the wise old man. Now what?*

*The man sent the snake back, telling him to show his
mighty fangs and flex his muscles but not to squirt venom and
injure people. This time around, the villagers kept a respectful
distance, sensing the snake's might as it slowly slithered into*

the village. Nothing happened, but everybody knew it was a distinct possibility.

TIME-OUT AT HOME
Practicing Kindness

Go out and do something kind today for your teenage child, yourself, and/or somebody else: carry a bag, hold the door, assist someone with something difficult, say a friendly word, or do a good deed. Note what happens.

Smile at everybody you encounter today, including yourself: at the shopping mall, in a traffic jam, by the coffee machine at work, or even when you have been waiting at an outpatients' clinic for an hour. Not only does a smile do wonders for the people around you, but it also has an effect on your brain. Smiling makes you feel happy, and this in turn attracts more happiness.

At moments when you feel hurt or frustrated, notice your mood and the way you tend to react. Observe your animosity, your tendency to want to get back at the other person. There is no need to do anything about this tendency to react. Just follow the many thoughts of revenge or retaliation for a while. And if those thoughts threaten to get the better of you, be like the snake. A bit of fierce hissing won't do any harm. Take a look around you, at home, at work, or perhaps next door, at someone who often annoys you, someone you dislike or try to avoid. Now spend the day looking for tenderness, generosity, and kindness in that person and write down your findings. But do it quietly, without that person's noticing.

fourteen

TRUSTING HAPPINESS

Happiness and love are basic needs. Nothing survives without love. Those who were physically, mentally, or emotionally neglected in childhood will have to make a concerted effort as adults to feel happy. Happiness is like a language that you learned during your early years that you now speak fluently. But even if this is not the case, you can still learn to cultivate happiness.

"I love you so much," my two-year-old son told me as he wrapped himself around me like a little capuchin monkey. *I love you so much*, I think as I look at my grown-up children thirty years later. They have become such happy people; they have become their own persons, pursuing their dreams, during journeys that were exhilarating, unplanned, and surprising, to say the least.

These wonders will never cease if we continue to open up to happiness and if we are aware of the happiness that we encounter on our path. As soon as you are in the now, happiness can find you, first here, then there. Mindfulness can help you to be present in this happiness—not by looking for it, but by simply experiencing it at every moment and enjoying it immensely while it lasts. Sometimes these moments will be very brief or precipitated by something superficial.

Tonight my happiness is profound, poignant, and above all completely new. My daughter is having a baby, and I am invited to be present at the birth, together with her boyfriend.

Night falls early. The stars are bright in the sky. It is January and it's freezing cold. The phone rings. It is John, Anne's partner, asking me to come to the hospital; the gentle waiting has begun. There is a deep, serene calm in the softly illuminated delivery room. There is a connection. All three of us breathe in and out simultaneously. The time has come. There is no future, no past, just an all-pervasive now. The panting and waves of pain suddenly swell and then subside again in the depths of yet unconscious life. They swell again, the age-old groans. You're a mother. I'm here with you. We're closer than ever. The final wave carries him to us. New. He who has never seen before looks at us. His open eyes are clear. It is infinitely tender and whole, this love at first sight. This is perfect happiness.

"Happiness enables us to breathe in particles of eternity," says the French psychiatrist Christophe André. Time stands still, and for a brief moment we feel immortal. Meditation has the same effect. Happiness and meditation both enable you to live in the now instead of lingering on the regret over what never was, what never will be, or what really ought to happen soon. Being happy is a lot like learning to play a musical instrument. By practicing a little bit every day, you improve without having to think about what is supposed to improve.

What is happiness? Happiness consists of brief moments of great simplicity when you experience something as exactly right. It appears out of nowhere, suddenly, without any effort on your part. We encounter it unexpectedly and in its full splendor. It was there all along, but we simply did not pay any attention to it. We are often too busy, hurried, or inattentive to the many moments of happiness. Or else we rush past it. In fact, we cover vast distances to find it and desperately cling to it when it threatens to slip through our fingers. Or we grow sad at the mere thought that this wonderful moment will pass. Of course happiness will pass, but for that very reason it is important to enjoy the moment. And these moments happen more often than we think.

It is three-thirty in the morning. Nesta, our eleven-month-old grandson, wakes up. My brain, still fuzzy with jetlag after the flight from Hong Kong, is trying to keep up with his great enthusiasm. Totally oblivious to time or clock, he is having his own little moment. Thoughts like "Oh no, not now, not this early" and kind, gentle words like "Nesta, sweetie, go back to sleep, it's far too early" have the opposite effect. He is roaring with delight. It takes awhile before my fog has cleared. But then I see it. I see his cause for pleasure. He is standing! Swaying unsteadily but triumphantly on his little crooked legs, he laughs and bares his two small front teeth. He is standing! For the first time, first thing in the morning. Who would have thought?

A new world has opened up to him, and he does not intend to lie down again. The standing turns into a wild dance around his bed. The bed itself is having a great time, too, its short plastic legs dancing along cautiously. And so together they move across the room. The entire performance lasts ninety minutes, and Henk and I occupy our front-row seats with bated breath. Such happiness, so early in the morning!

Being courageously present in every moment, day and night, can help us to enjoy the hundreds of chances for happiness that are available in our day. It also helps us cope in more troubled times, when we are beset by stress, pain, fear, or uncertainty. Happiness and unhappiness go hand in hand, forming an indivisible reality, like light and shadow. But the true secret of happiness lies in noticing that you are happy when you are. You do not have to look for it, there is nothing to cling to or let go of, and there is no need to think you will never be happy again. Just noticing that you are happy when you are is enough.

I wish you and your teenage child or children many mindful moments of happiness, in the midst of your day-to-day worries, stacks of laundry, unsolved problems, or feelings of distress. A warm smile, a comforting hand, or getting suddenly lifted up in the air by your incredibly tall teenage child works wonders. For all of us. Happiness appears out of nowhere, and as such, it is always present within us. Isn't it wonderful to know this?

AFTERWORD

My mother has given me the trust and great honor to write the epilogue to this wonderful book. As you will have noticed, my adolescence was not easy. Not for me as a teenager, and certainly not for my parents. Thinking back on those years, self-confidence and being true to myself were the hardest things for me. Trust, both in myself and in others, was a frequent topic of conversation. How can you trust others when you do not know where to find it within yourself? How can you trust yourself when you keep making mistakes or the wrong decisions?

These were some of the many questions I kept asking myself. To me, trust was something that had nothing to do with me. I often acted like I was bursting with confidence, but I never truly felt it. Similarly, I distrusted many of the people around me. My father, Henk, and my mother did have faith in me, and even when things were going completely wrong, they recognized a strength in me that was invisible to me. Their trust in me inspired me to travel and discover who I was and what I might like and be able to do. This trust allowed me to develop into a person I am proud of. It has taught me that I may not always make the correct decision or take the right road, but that as a person I am perfect as I am. Their confidence in me has given me the most precious gift imaginable. It has given me self-confidence.

Puberty is an incredibly difficult period for many young people, as they and sometimes their environment undergo big changes. My parents' belief that my good qualities outweighed the bad made a world of difference to me, so I hope this book can inspire and support parents and their teenage children in difficult moments or situations.

If one advances confidently in the direction of his dreams, and endeavors to live the life he has imagined, he will meet with a success unexpected in common hours.

—*Henry David Thoreau*

Mom, thank you for your faith in my dreams at moments when it must have been far from easy for you as a mother. Now that I am a mother myself, I hope to pass this gift on to my own children. I have learned so much from you, and I hope to do so for many more years to come.

—*Anne*

BIBLIOGRAPHY

Brown, Brené C. *Daring Greatly: How the Courage to Be Vulnerable Transforms the Way We Live, Love, Parent, and Lead*. New York: Penguin, 2013.

Chödrön, Pema. *Verzacht je hart*. Utrecht: Ten Have, 2011.

Feldman, Christina. *Beginner's Guide to Buddhist Meditation: Practices for Mindful Living*. Berkeley, CA: Rodmell Press, 2006.

Jenson, Jean. *Reclaiming Your Life: A Step-by-Step Guide to Using Regression Therapy to Overcome the Effects of Childhood Abuse*. New York: Meridian, 1996.

Judith, Anodea. *Wheels of Life: The Classic Guide to the Chakra System*. Woodbury, MN: Llewellyn Publications, 1987.

Kabat-Zinn, Jon. *Full Catastrophe Living: How to Cope with Stress, Pain, and Illness Using Mindfulness Meditation*. Rev. ed. New York: Bantam Books, 2013.

Kabat-Zinn, Myla, and Jon Kabat-Zinn. *Everyday Blessings: The Inner Work of Mindful Parenting*. New York: Hyperion, 1998.

Neff, Kristin. *Self-Compassion*. New York: HarperCollins, 2011.

Rumi. "The Guest House." In *The Rumi Collection: An Anthology of Translations by Jevlâna Jalâluddin Rumi*, ed. Kabir Helminski (Boston: Shambhala Publications, 1998).

Santorelli, Saki. "Putting Yourself in Someone Else's Shoes" exercise. In *Heal Thy Self: Lessons on Mindfulness in Medicine*. New York: Crown Publications, 2000.

Siegel, Daniel. *Mindsight: Transform Your Brain with the New Science of Kindness*. London: One World Publications, 2011.

Snel, Eline. Exercises from "Attention Matters!" Handbook 4 for Teens. In *Mindfulness for Teens*. Self-published, 2013.

———. *Sitting Still Like a Frog: Mindfulness Exercises for Kids (and Their Parents)*. Boston: Shambhala Publications, 2014.

ACKNOWLEDGMENTS

Writing and teaching mindfulness programs for adults, children, and teenagers is a lifelong process of development. A great many people have played an important role in this process as sources of inspiration and guides, keeping alive and clarifying the principles of mindfulness in daily life, both for me and for the people I work with on a daily basis. It is a privilege to share parents' and teenagers' day-to-day efforts to understand themselves and, where possible, change bad habits. I am always touched when young people confide in me their ideals, despair, resilience, and triumphs—and to see them carve out their own unique path toward adulthood, whatever happens. By being there for them, by sharing mindful moments, I have been witness to remarkable transformations.

I would like to thank the many schools, teachers, parents, and teenagers who have had the courage to take part in the Attention Matters! programs in school or in my practice. Without their presence, sense of humor, and positive feedback, I could never have written this book. Likewise, my children and grandchildren are a daily source of inspiration to me. They teach me, time and time again, that nothing in the adventurous process of growing up can be taken for granted.

In particular, I would like to thank my daughter, Anne Marlijn, for her courage and for allowing me to be open about everything we went through together during her teenage years.

As always, my husband, Henk, read every word I wrote. With his natural wisdom and constructive criticism he never fails to simplify, clarify, and improve my writing. He also gives me space while still being close. And that means the world to me.

I would like to thank Marijke and Wichert, the owners of a beautiful campside at La Montagne, where I had the peace to write my books; my colleagues Patries Dekker, Chris te Riele, and Irene Willemsen; Yolanda Derksen; and my writing coach Tanny Dobbelaar for reading the first rough drafts of this book. Their kind words and professional approach encouraged me to continue. I would also like to thank my publisher, Regine Dugardyn, and everybody else at Ten Have for giving me the opportunity to embark on this second adventure in writing. They supported and accompanied me on this journey with dedication and patience.

Without the enthusiastic and international team of colleagues at the International Academy for Mindful Teaching, I would not have been able to write this book. They are always there, ready to bring mindfulness and teaching together and to maintain the child-training program at a consistently high professional—and heartful—level.

I would like to thank Professor R. H. J. Scholte of the Department of Orthopedagogy at the Behavioural Science Institute at Radboud University in Nijmegen, Netherlands, for his faith and continued support for carrying out research in schools into the effect of Attention Matters! on learning and concentration. Our collaboration is always open, warm, and innovative.

I owe special thanks to Jonathan Green, Beth Frankl, and Kay Campbell of Shambhala Publications. Their commitment, creativity, and enthusiasm have resulted in a wonderful edition of this book.

RESOURCES

For more information, see the following websites:

www.academyformindfulteaching.com
www.elinesnel.com

"Sitting Still," a mindfulness app created by the author for teenagers, is available for iPhone and Android. It includes meditations and guided techniques specifically designed for young people. Sara Marlowe recorded the "voice" of the app in a mindful way, and young people will appreciate her warmth and tone. I am very grateful for her contribution.

The links to purchase this app are:

https://itunes.apple.com/us/app/sitting-still
/id891207446?mt=8
https://play.google.com/store/apps/details?id=se.lichten
stein.mind.sitting.still.en

ABOUT THE AUTHOR

Eline Snel (b. 1954) has been working as an independent therapist and trainer since 1980. In 1990 she started developing meditation- and mindfulness-training programs. As a certified mindfulness and compassion trainer, she has been teaching adults, children, and teenagers for many years. She is the founder and owner of the International Academy for Mindful Teaching, where she teaches the mindfulness-training program Mindfulness Matters! to kids and teens as well as to educators and mental-health-care professionals. The program is taught in the Netherlands, various European countries, and Hong Kong. She works with her daughter and a great team of other inspired professionals.

Eline has developed four training handbooks for the age range five to nineteen, which are widely used in both elementary and high schools, mental-health institutions, rehabilitation centers, and trainers' own practices. More than six thousand children have attended the Mindfulness Matters! program. Her best-selling book *Sitting Still Like a Frog: Mindfulness Exercises for Kids (and Their Parents)* has been translated into more than twelve languages.